Customs of Japan
日本のしきたり
a photographic overview

IBC パブリッシング編

IBC

Copyright©2016 IBC Publishing, Inc.

●

Photographs by

Gorazd Vilhar   p.47(下), 55, 59, 91, 99, 103, 121, 123, 129, 173, 191, 193, 195

Katsuhiko Mizuno   p.69, 87, 131, 135, 137, 145

Katsuhiko Mizuno and Hidehiko Mizuno   p.15, 19, 23, 33, 45, 50, 57, 81, 83, 93, 107, 125, 147, 149, 159, 161, 163, 167, 169, 177, 179, 181, 199

Nishihama/Shutterstock.com   p.39

Sakamoto Kenji   p.153

sasaken/Shutterstock.com   p.37

Shuichi Yamagata   p.165, 171, 175

Toshinobu Takeuchi   p.21, 25, 35, 77, 101, 115, 117

©HIDEAKI TANAKA/SEBUN PHOTO/amanaimages   p.17

©JAPACK/orion/amanaimages   p.95

©YUKIO TANAKA / SEBUN PHOTO / amanaimages   p.201

●

Illustrations by Ted Takahashi   p.132, 133, 138–143

●

Text by Haruhito Tsuchiya

except Chapter 6 by Yoji Yamakuse

Translation by Ginny Tapley Takemori

except Preface by James M. Vardaman, Chapter 6 by Michael A. Cooney

●

Design by Kei Saito from Buddha Productions

●

All rights reserved, No part of this book may be reproduced in any form without written permission from the publisher.

First Edition 2016

ISBN 978-4-7946-0418-7

Printed in Japan

Customs of Japan
日本のしきたり
a photographic overview

IBC パブリッシング 編

はじめに

　自分の考えや能力を強く主張することなく社会を運営してゆくために、日本人が発展させてきたものが「しきたり」という社会システムです。

　古代から、農業での豊作を神に感謝し、人と人との絆を強くするために、人々はさまざまな儀式をつくってゆきました。その後、身分や階級制度が社会に浸透する中で、さらに人と人との上下関係を具体的に表すための作法やマナーが生み出されます。

　儀式や作法は、すべての人がその様式に従うために、それぞれの場での行動様式、すなわち、型が生み出され、次第に社会の多くの場面で、さまざまな型を「しきたり」として尊重するようになったのです。

　「しきたり」はいまでは、日本人の生活様式、行動のいたるところに見ることができます。ビジネスでの名刺交換、相撲での取組前の儀式、そしてごく日常でいうならば、お酒の席での杯の受け方や注ぎ方など。

　いまとなっては、古くさえ思える「しきたり」の中にも、実は現代人の心の奥に残り、形を変えて影響を与えているものがあります。あるいは、その「しきたり」によって行動するがゆえに、海外の人との間に誤解が生まれそうなものなど、あらゆる角度からそれらを見つめてゆくことが必要な時代になってきているのかもしれません。

　本書をご一読いただき、そして、自らの経験や体験を取り込んで、自分の言葉としていかに日本の「しきたり」を海外の人たちに伝えてゆくか、読者の方々にご一考いただければ幸甚です。

IBCパブリッシング編集部

Preface

In order to administer the affairs of society without asserting an individual's ideas or capacities, the Japanese developed a social system that is referred to as *shikitari*. In this volume, we call them "Customs of Japan".

In agriculture from ancient times, the Japanese developed various ceremonies in order to express gratitude to the deities for an abundant harvest and to strengthen bonds between individuals. Later, as social standing and the class system permeated society, rules of etiquette and manners evolved as a way of giving concrete form to the hierarchical relations between people.

Rituals and rules of etiquette became formalized into patterns, called *kata*, so that everyone would recognize the proper way to behave in each distinct situation. Eventually these proper patterns of behavior came to be broadly regarded as customary practices.

Such conventions can still be observed among the Japanese today in their patterns of daily life and behavior. Traditional etiquette can be seen in the business world in the way people exchange business cards, in sumo in the rituals that precede the bouts, and, in an everyday situation, in the way people pour saké for one another at a drinkery.

Today, even among those who think of these traditional rules of etiquette as outdated, such conventions of behavior remain just below the surface, although in somewhat modified forms. Further, as a result of behaving according to traditional forms of manners, it sometimes happens that misunderstandings occur in interactions between Japanese and people from other countries. For these various reasons, it is important to reexamine these customs from a variety of perspectives.

It is our hope that you will read this volume, reflect on your own personal experience, and give some thought to exactly how you might explain customs of Japan to people from abroad.

IBC Publishing Editorial Department

Contents 目次

Preface はじめに **4**

Chapter 1 第1章
Annual Events 年間行事 **11**

1. New Year... 12 　　　　　　　　　　　お正月
2. *Setsubun*: The End of Winter... 16 　　節　分
3. *Ohanami*: Blossom Viewing... 20 　　お花見
4. Seasonal Festivals... 22 　　　　　　　節　句
5. *Ohigan*: Equinoctial Weeks... 34 　　 お彼岸
6. *Doyō*: The Hottest Part of Summer... 36 　夏の土用
7. Obon... 40 　　　　　　　　　　　　お　盆
8. *Otsukimi*: Moon Viewing... 44 　　　お月見
9. *Omatsuri*: Festivals... 46 　　　　　　お祭り
10. *Ōmisoka*: New Year's Eve... 48 　　 大晦日

Chapter 2 第2章
Life Events 人生 **53**

1. Birth... 54 　出　産
2. *Shichi-go-san*: Childhood Milestones... 58 　七五三
3. Coming of Age... 60 　成　人
4. Long-life Celebrations... 62 　賀　寿
5. *Yakudoshi*: Unlucky Years... 64 　厄　年

Chapter 3 第3章
Weddings, Funerals, and Religions 婚礼/葬儀/宗教 **67**

1. Engagement... 68 　婚　約
2. The Wedding Ceremony and Reception... 70 　結婚式と披露宴
3. Auspicious and Unlucky Days... 76 　式日/六曜
4. Funerals... 80 　葬　儀
5. Gods and the Buddha... 84 　神と仏
6. Folk Beliefs... 90 　民間信仰

Chapter 4 第4章
Social Events つき合い 105

1. Mid-year and Year-end Gifts... 106 — お中元/お歳暮
2. Seating Etiquette... 108 — 上座/下座
3. *Enkai*: Parties... 112 — 宴会
4. *Aisatsu*: Greeting People... 114 — あいさつ
5. Greetings Cards at New Year and in Summer... 116 — 年賀状/暑中見舞い

Chapter 5 第5章
Clothes, Food, and Homes 衣・食・住 119

1. Kimonos and Accessories... 120 — 着物・小物
2. Japanese Food... 126 — 和　食
3. Homes... 134 — 家
4. Lifestyle... 144 — 暮らし方

Column... 132, 138

Chapter 6 第6章
Soul of Japan 日本人のこころ **151**

1. Harmony... 152 — 和
2. Form, Way of Doing Things... 156 — 型
3. Energy... 160 — 気
4. Feelings... 162 — 情
5. Loyalty... 172 — 忠
6. The Gods... 174 — 神
7. Buddhism... 180 — 仏

Chapter 7 第7章
Miscellaneous その他 **183**

1. Attracting Luck... 184 — 縁起かつぎ
2. Iconography... 190 — 図像
3. Leisure... 194 — レジャー
4. Hobbies... 198 — 趣味

Index... 202

第 1 章
Chapter 1

年間行事
Annual Events

お正月	❶	New Year
節 分	❷	*Setsubun*: The End of Winter
お花見	❸	*Ohanami*: Blossom Viewing
節 句	❹	Seasonal Festivals
お彼岸	❺	*Ohigan*: Equinoctial Weeks
夏の土用	❻	*Doyō*: The Hottest Part of Summer
お 盆	❼	Obon
お月見	❽	*Otsukimi*: Moon Viewing
お祭り	❾	*Omatsuri*: Festivals
大晦日	❿	*Ōmisoka*: New Year's Eve

1 New Year
お正月

Preparing to welcome the new gods

According to Shinto belief, New Year is the time when the *kami,* or gods, **bring good fortune** to homes. To this end, families clean their houses, decorate their *kamidana* (**altar to the gods**), and place a *kadomatsu* pine decoration by the front entrance. The *kamidana* is decorated with fresh *sakaki* leaves and a new *shimenawa* rope to indicate the **sacred space** where the *kami* may approach. The *kagami mochi,* made with a small, round rice cake placed on top of a larger round rice cake, is an essential **offering** to the *kami.* Mochi rice cakes are a traditional food made from polished white rice, and also considered a symbol of a **good harvest**. The *kagami mochi,* literally "mirror mochi," is given its round shape and name after the bronze mirror that is one of the **Three Sacred Treasures**, and it can be placed on the *kamidana,* or in another sacred space at the heart of the home such the *tokonoma* alcove.

新しい神様をお迎えする準備

　日本の神道では、正月になると**福をもたらす**神様が家々にやってくると考えられた。そこでそれぞれの家庭では**神棚**を飾り、家の中をきれいにし、玄関には目印となる松の飾り物（門松）を置いた。神棚の飾りで大事なのは<ruby>榊<rt>さかき</rt></ruby>の葉としめ縄を新しくすることで、そこが神様の寄り付く**神聖な場所**となる。神様への**供え物**としては大小の丸い餅を重ねた「鏡餅」が欠かせない。餅は米をついて作る伝統食品であり、**豊穣**のシンボルともされる。それを丸い形にして「鏡餅」と呼ぶのは、**三種の神器**の一つである「銅鏡」に見立てるからで、神棚以外にも「床の間」など家の中心となる神聖な場所にも置かれる。

Chapter 1 Annual Events

Osechi ryōri: special dishes prepared for New Year

The dishes that grace the dinner table for the first three days of the year are known as *osechi ryōri*. These are made from **ingredients** considered auspicious, such as prawns, **herring roe**, and black beans, that are seasoned and preserved, and arranged pleasingly in stacking boxes known as *jūbako*. The contents vary between eastern and western Japan, but it is a lot of work to make at home so these days people purchase sets made by famous food brands and sold in department stores, convenience stores and on the Internet. Housewives do prepare some other dishes such as *zōni*, a soup containing mochi rice cakes and fish or chicken, and *otoso*, sake infused with herbs, but on the whole they are saved the trouble of cooking during this period. However, many people **get bored of** eating the same things for every meal over three days.

正月に食べるのは「おせち料理」

　元旦から3日ぐらいまでの間、食卓を飾るのは「おせち料理」である。えびや**数の子**、黒豆など縁起が良いとされる**食材**を使って保存できるように味付けし、重箱にきれいに盛り付けたものである。関東と関西では中身が異なるが、自宅で作るのは大変なので、近年では有名料理店ブランドのものが、デパートやコンビニやネット通販などで手に入る。ほかには、餅と魚や鶏肉などを入れた吸い物（雑煮）や薬草酒（お屠蘇）を用意するが、基本的に主婦は台所仕事はしなくてすむから大助かりだ。でも、3日間の3食がこればかりでは**飽きてしまう**人も多い。

Chapter 1　Annual Events

② *Setsubun*: The End of Winter
節分

Bean scattering: "Fortune in and demons out!"

On February 3, *setsubun* events are held all over Japan. This is the day before *risshun,* the first day of spring, and marks the change in the season. At shrines and temples as well as individual houses, people scatter roasted beans while chanting **"Fortune in and demons out!"** This is to attract happiness into the house and drive out evil spirits. Since the beans are thrown at the evil spirits, they are roasted to ensure they do not sprout later. The custom is said to have derived from an event to drive out demons held at the Imperial Court on New Year's Eve, which later spread amongst the populace. People also eat the same number of beans as their age (or sometimes one extra) to drive evil spirits out of their body.

豆をまいて「福は内、鬼は外」

　毎年2月の3日頃になると、日本各地で「節分」の行事が行われる。この日は「立春」(春が始まるという意味)の前日であり、「節分」は季節の分かれ目との意味になる。その行事というのは、寺社やそれぞれの家で、「**福は内、鬼は外！**」と掛け声をかけながら炒った豆をまくのである。掛け声は「福＝幸福は家の中に入れ、鬼＝邪気は外に出ろ」という意味で、豆は邪気にぶつけるツブテだから、後で芽が出ないように炒ってあるのだ。もともとは宮中で大晦日に行われていた「鬼はらい」の行事が民間に広まったものといわれる。また、人々はその豆を年齢の数だけ (あるいは1つ余計に) 食べることで体内の邪気もはらう。

Chapter 1 Annual Events

17

In fact, there are twenty-four *setsubun* every year

Japan's climate has four distinct seasons. Therefore, while you have the start of spring, you also have **junctures** for summer, autumn, and winter. Each of the four seasons have six further divisions, which means you therefore have a total of twenty-four seasonal changes. Since *setsubun* means literally "change in season," this means there are twenty-four *setsubun*. These are collectively known as *nijūshi sekki* (**twenty-four divisions of the solar year**). In addition to the **spring** and **autumn equinoxes**, when the day and night are the same length, there is *daikan*, which is the coldest period of the year, *taisho*, which is the hottest period, and some with poetic names like *keichitsu*, or **awakening of insects**, which is when bugs emerge from **hibernation**, and *hakuro*, or **white dew**, which is when the air cools and condenses as dew. However, the fact that the only *setsubun* celebrated now is the one marking the end of winter is probably due the joy felt at the end of winter and regeneration of life at the start of spring.

本当は１年に24もある「節分」

　日本の気候は四季がはっきりしている。だから春の始まり（立春）もあれば、夏も秋も冬もそれぞれの区切りがある。四季はさらに6つずつの**区切り**があるので合計で24もの「節分」があることになる。これを「**二十四節気**」と呼ぶ。昼と夜の時間が等しい**春分、秋分**とか、最も寒い「**大寒**」、暑いのが「**大暑**」、**冬ごもり**していた虫が顔を出す「**啓蟄**」、大気が冷えて結露する「**白露**」など詩的な名前もついている。これは陰暦にもとづく農事の目安だった。それぞれに行事もあったはずだ。しかし立春前の「節分」行事だけが継承されてきたのは、冬を経て迎えた春こそが生命再生のスタートとして喜ばれたからかもしれない。

3 *Ohanami*: Blossom Viewing
お花見

"The cherry among flowers, the samurai among men"

When the cold winter passes and cheerful spring arrives, people's spirits rise too. Especially when the cherries bloom, which is when Japanese people **itch to** attend *ohanami*, or blossom viewing parties. The Chinese may prefer the earlier plum and peach blossoms, but for the Japanese blossom viewing can only refer to cherry blossoms. This is how much we as a nation love them. The fifteenth century Zen Buddhist priest Ikkyū Sōjun also said that for him the most agreeable things were, "The cherry among flowers; the samurai among men; the **sea bream** among fish; the **maple leaf** among kimono patterns…"

Ohanami is not just about viewing blossoms. It is about enjoying time with friends and colleagues drinking sake, eating picnic fare, and singing songs beneath the blossoms.

「花は桜木、人は武士」

　寒い冬が過ぎてうららかな春がやってくると、人々の心も浮き立ってくる。とくに桜の花が咲きだすと、日本人は「お花見」に出かけたくなる**うずうずする**。これが中国人ならもう少し早く咲く梅や桃の花なのだろうが、日本人は桜を見に出かけることだけを「お花見」という。それほどまでに桜が大好きな国民である。15世紀（室町時代）に活躍した禅宗の高僧である一休宗純も、「花は桜木、人は武士、魚は**鯛**、小袖（の模様）は**もみじ**…」が、一番好ましいものだと言った。

　お花見は花を観賞するだけではない。気の合う人たちと、桜の木の下で酒を飲んだり、持ち寄ったご馳走を食べたり、歌ったりして楽しむことがお花見である。

Chapter 1 Annual Events

4 Seasonal Festivals
節句

Five particular festivals during the year

Numbers were important in the **yin-yang ideology** of ancient China, with **even numbers** considered **stable** and **static**, and therefore yin, while **odd numbers** are unstable and dynamic and therefore yang. Odd numbers (yang) were considered luckier, but yang plus yang become yin and more **prone to** bring about misfortune. This is why specific odd-numbered days in odd-numbered months are emphasized and events held to **ward off misfortune**. Since these also coincide with changes in the season, they are also called *sekku* (or sometimes *sechie*), "seasonal festivals." The largest yang number is 9, so if we discount November (the eleventh month) and only count the other odd-numbered months, there are five of these seasonal festivals during the year. The Edo-period shogunate celebrated these *gosekku* (five seasonal festivals) with specific events for each that have become **ingrained in** Japanese culture.

１年間に５日、固有の行事がある節句

　古代中国の**陰陽思想**には数字への信仰がある。**偶数**は**安定して静的**であるので陰の数字、**奇数**は不安定で動的であることから陽の数字とされ、奇数（陽）の方が縁起が良いとされた。しかし陽と陽が重なると陰に**転じ**厄災を生じやすくなる。それが１年間の奇数月の特定の奇数日を重視することになり、**厄を払う**行事を行うようになった。季節の節目でもあることから「節句」（節供あるいは節会とも）と呼ばれるようになった。陽の数字の最大は９なので11月を除くと１年に５日の「節句」があることになり、日本では江戸幕府が五節句の祝日とし、それぞれの行事が**根付く**ことになった。

January 7: *Jinjitsu*, or "Day of Mankind"

In ancient China, the first seven days of the first month were designated rooster, dog, boar, sheep, ox, horse, and human, and the fortune of the year was divined according to the weather on those days. Further, it was decreed that on these days the animal concerned should not be harmed, and on the seventh day (for humans), criminals would go unpunished. There was also the custom of eating a hot soup containing seven different herbs, a practice which reached Japan, where it has become the day to eat *nanakusa-gayu* (rice gruel with seven herbs).

1月7日は「人日の節句」

古代中国では1月のはじめの7日間に、鶏、犬、豚、羊、牛、馬、人を割り当て、その天候からその年のそれぞれの吉凶を占った。またその日はその動物を食べてはならない日とされ、人の日（人日）つまり1月7日は罪人の処罰をしない日とされた。またこの日は7種類の野草を入れた羹（テリーヌ）を食べる習慣もあった。これが日本に伝わってからは、「七草がゆ」を食べる日となった。

Chapter 1 Annual Events

25

March 3: *Jōshi*, or "First Day of the Snake"

In China, on the first Day of the Snake in the third month, a ceremony would be conducted on the banks of a stream to drive away ill fortune, and parties known as "winding stream banquets" would be held in which participants had to compose a poem before a wine cup floating on the current reached them. This was also introduced into the Imperial Court in Japan. It was around this time that a human figure cut out of paper began to be used in the ceremony to banish ill fortune, and this developed into the *hina matsuri* "Dolls Festival" for girls that is widely celebrated today. It is also known as the Peach Festival, named after the blossoms that bloom at this time.

3月3日は「上巳の節句」

　中国では3月上旬の巳の日、川のほとりで厄を払う儀式を行ったり、水に浮かべた盃が自分のところに着くまでに歌を詠む「曲水の宴」を行った。日本の宮中にも取り入れられた。そのうち厄払いの部分を紙で作った人形で行うようになり、女の子の「ひな祭り」にと変形して庶民の間にも広がった。この季節に咲く花から「桃の節句」ともいう。

May 5: *Tango*, or "First Day of the Horse"

In China, *chimaki* rice dumplings wrapped in bamboo leaves are eaten on the first Day of the Horse of the fifth month. According to legend this is the day on which, in the third century BC, the senior Chu statesman Qu Yuan became so anguished after his fall from power that he drowned himself, and his followers threw *chimaki* dumplings into the water to distract the fish from eating his body, and **held a memorial service** for him. There was also a custom whereby misfortune was driven out with **irises** and **mugwort** leaves. In the Kamakura period, it was known as *shōbu no hi* or "day of the iris" (*shōbu* is a homophone for "iris" and "military prowess") and was a day for boys, celebrated with displays of warrior dolls. Later still, the Chinese legend of a carp that succeeded in climbing a waterfall to become a dragon developed into the custom of hanging out **carp streamers**.

5月5日は「端午の節句」

　5月の始め（端）の午の日は、中国では「ちまき」を食べる。紀元前3世紀の楚の重臣だった屈原が失脚して悲嘆のあまり入水自殺した日だが、屈原を慕う人々が遺体が魚に食べられぬようにちまきを投げ込んで**供養した**との伝説がある。また**菖蒲**や**よもぎ**の葉で邪気を払う風習もあったという。日本では鎌倉時代に「菖蒲（武を貴ぶ尚武と同じ読み）の節句」つまり男の子の節句とされるようになり武者人形を飾るようになったという。またのちには、滝をのぼる鯉が龍になるという中国の出世伝説も取り入れて、**鯉幟**を立てる風習も加わった。

Chapter 1 Annual Events

July 7: *Tanabata*, or the "Star Festival"

In the heavens two lovers, a cowherd and a weaver maid, dwell either side of the Milky Way. The Lord of Heaven had **taken pity on** the hardworking couple and allowed them to marry, but they were so happy that the weaver maid forgot about her weaving. **In a rage**, the Lord of Heaven separated them and thenceforth allowed them to meet only once a year. This Chinese legend is linked also to the *kikkōden* festival to pray for **dexterity** in needlework and to Obon traditions. Since arriving in Japan, it has become an event where people write wishes for handicraft skills and good relationships on strips of paper that they hang on bamboo grass.

7月7日は「七夕の節句」

天の河を挟んで片方には牛飼いの牽牛という男がおり、他方に蚕から糸を紡いで天女の衣を織る織女がいた。働きづめの二人を**憐れんだ**天帝が結婚を許したが幸せのあまり織女は機織りを忘れた。**怒った**天帝は二人を引き離し、1年に1度しか会えなくした。これが中国の「棚機伝説」であり、裁縫の**上達**を祈る乞巧奠行事やお盆行事とも結びついた。日本に入ってからは技芸の上達や良縁を願った短冊を笹の葉に結んで飾る「七夕」の行事になった。

September 9: *Chōyō,* or the "Chrysanthemum Festival"

Nine is the highest yang number. When doubled, it changes to yin and is capable of attracting great misfortune. Customs to dispel this misfortune and pray for **longevity** included drinking sake on which the season's flower, the chrysanthemum, had been floated, and wiping one's body with cotton steeped in dew from chrysanthemums. There was also a custom (called *tōkō,* or "climbing to a height") of dangling a bag of Japanese pepper from one's arm, taking chrysanthemum-scented sake, and going to a small hill outside town for a picnic. According to the newspaper *People's China*, the *tōkō* tradition has gone out of fashion in China, but the Chrysanthemum Festival has become important as a day of respect for the aged. In Japan, **vestiges** of the festival remain in the name of the Nagasaki Kunchi Festival (*kunchi* originally meant ninth day) and the Okinawan *awamori* (rice brandy) called "Chrysanthemum Dew."

9月9日は「重陽の節句」

　9は最大の陽の数字。それが重なると陰に転じ大きな災厄を招きかねない。その厄を払って**長寿**を祈るために、季節の花である菊を酒に浮かべて飲んだり、菊の露をしみこませた綿で体をぬぐうといった習慣が行われていた。また、茱萸の袋を腕に結び、菊の香の酒を持って郊外の小高い丘（天に近い！）にピクニックに出かける習慣（登高）もあった。「登高」以外の伝統がすたれた現代中国では、重陽節を「老人節」、または「敬老節」として重視するようになったと「人民中国」紙は報じている。日本では、長崎くんち（9日）という祭りの名前と沖縄の泡盛「菊の露」にその**名残り**がある。

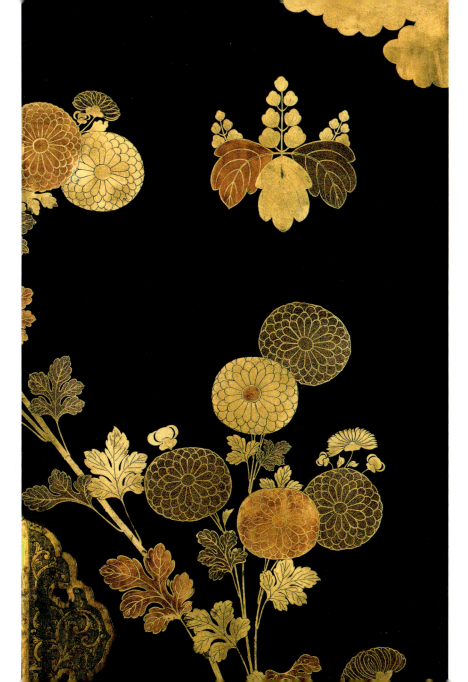

5 *Ohigan*: Equinoctial Weeks
お彼岸

Two annual visits to the graves of ancestors

There are two days every year when day and night are the same length. The Spring Equinox (around March 21) and Autumn Equinox (around September 23) are **movable national holidays** in Japan. The three days before and after the equinoctial days, seven days in all, are called *ohigan*, when it is customary for people to visit the graves of their ancestors. This custom is not practiced in other Buddhist countries.

Also, due to the major changes in temperature around the time of *ohigan*, there is a saying, "**Neither heat nor cold lasts beyond the equinox**."

The word *ohigan* comes from the Buddhist term for "the other world" (or afterlife, as opposed to *shigan*, "this world"), where the other world is a paradise in which we are freed of **earthly desires**, while this life is full of suffering and **delusion**. Our ancestors, having passed away, live in the other world.

年に２度、先祖の墓参りをする日

　昼と夜の長さが同じになる日が年間に２度ある。春の春分の日（３月21日頃）と秋の秋分の日（９月23日頃）で、国民の**移動祝日**になっている。これらの日を挟んだ前後３日、計７日間が「お彼岸」で、先祖の墓参りをする習慣がある。これはほかの仏教圏にはない。

　また、このお彼岸辺りから気温が大きく変化することから、「**暑さ寒さも彼岸まで**」ということわざもある。

　お彼岸という言葉は仏教用語の「彼岸／此岸」から来たもので、**煩悩**を脱した極楽の世界が彼岸、苦しみと**迷い**に満ちた現世が此岸。死者である先祖は彼岸に暮らしている。

Chapter 1 Annual Events

Doyō: The Hottest Part of Summer
夏の土用

Eel boosts stamina in summer

According to the doctrine of yin yang and the five elements, the earth is made up of the five elements metal, wood, water, fire, and earth which change according to the season and influence our mood. Spring is wood, summer is fire, autumn is metal, and winter is water, while the dominant element at each turn of season is earth. However, this periodic dominance of earth has been largely forgotten, and now Japanese people are only concerned with its effect in the *doyō* season, the hottest part of summer before the start of fall (about eighteen days). This is because they believe in the power of a certain food to **boost stamina** in this hot, humid season when everyone lacks energy. It is particularly thought to be good to eat on the Day of the Ox that falls within the eighteen-day *doyō* period. That's right: fried eel served in a salt-sweet sauce!

It is also known that the catchphrase "Let's eat eel to get through summer!" was **coined** by the multitalented Hiraga Gennai (1728–1780), a botanist, popular novelist, inventor, and painter. However, these days when even catches of fish fry are persistently poor, eel is also becoming a delicacy beyond the reach of ordinary people.

夏のスタミナ補給には「ウナギ」

　陰陽五行の説によれば、世界は「木・火・土・金・水」の5つの成分で構成され、それぞれが季節によって交代しながら気を支配するという。春は木、夏は火、秋は金、冬は水であるが、その季節の変わり目ごとに支配的になるのが土である。しかし、そんな細切れに配

される土の気のことは忘れられて、立秋前の夏の土用(約18日間)だけが日本人の関心を集めるようになった。蒸し暑く、誰もが元気をなくす季節なのだが、特別な食べ物が**そのスタミナを補給してくれる**と信じられているからだ。この食べ物は、とくに土用18日間のうちの「丑の日」に食べるのが良いとされる。そう、甘辛いタレで焼いたウナギである。

　「ウナギを食べて夏を乗り切ろう」という宣伝文句を**考え出した**人物もわかっている。植物学者で戯作者で発明家で画家でもあったマルチタレントの平賀源内(1728-1780)だ。ただ、稚魚の不漁が続く昨今ではウナギも庶民の手が届かない高級品になっている。

⑦ Obon
お盆

Summer events to honor the spirits of the dead

Obon customs **vary** according to region, but are generally a series of events held from the 13th to the 16th of either July or August to welcome back the spirits of family members who have passed away, make offerings to them, and send them back again. Particular consideration is shown by getting a priest to **chant sutras** for them, especially for those who died within the past year, called *niibon*. Fires are commonly lit at the entrance to houses in the evening to welcome the spirits and to see them off again, but the ways of making offerings and decorating the memorial tablets and graves vary according to the Buddhist sect. In Pure Land and some other sects, offerings of horse or cow figurines made from cucumber or eggplant and **millet**, hanging Japanese lantern plants, and food placed on lotus leaves.

死者の霊を供養する夏の行事

　地方によって**異なる**が、7月または8月の13日から16日の間に、亡くなった祖先、家族の霊を迎え、供養し、送り返す一連の行事のこと。とくに亡くなって1年未満の死者の場合は「新盆」と称して、僧侶に**読経して**もらうなど手厚く供養する。霊を迎えたり、送る際には夕方に玄関などで火を炊くのが一般的だが、位牌や墓前への供養の仕方や飾りは仏教宗派によって異なるが、浄土宗などではきゅうりやナスと**キビ**がらで作った馬や牛を供えたり、ほおずきを吊るしたり、蓮の葉に食べ物を置いたりする。

Chapter 1 Annual Events

A national summer holiday and the *bon-odori* dance

Around August 15, many people take holidays and travel back to their hometown to visit the family home, effectively making it a national summer vacation. Also, on the 15th, at the height of Obon, a **scaffold platform** is set up on a vacant lot in the community, in the precincts of shrines or temples, or on school grounds, and the local people dance the *bon-odori* in a circle around it. People often sing local folk songs, and those returning from far away enjoy feeling nostalgic.

国民的夏休みと盆踊り

　新暦の8月15日前後は、夏の休暇を取る人、実家のある故郷に帰省する人が多いために、実質的に国民的な夏休みになっている。また、お盆の中日である15日あたりには、集落の空き地や寺社の境内、学校のグラウンドなどに櫓を組んで、それを囲むようにして回りながら踊る盆踊りが各地で催される。歌われるのがその地域に伝わる民謡だったりすることが多く、帰省した人々などはノスタルジックな気分を楽しめる。

⑧ *Otsukimi*: Moon Viewing
お月見

The difference between the Fifteenth Night and the Thirteenth Night

Under the old lunar calendar, autumn covered the period from the seventh to the ninth months. The mid-autumn moon comes right in the middle of this period, on the fifteenth of the eighth month, (the Fifteenth Night). This falls in September under the solar calendar, and moon-viewing events are called *otsukimi*, but unlike *ohanami* blossom viewing, do not involve drinking and feasting. There are displays of **pampas grass**, *tsukimi-dango* "full-moon dumplings," taro potatoes, and edamame. This was also a harvest festival, so another name for it is *imomeigetsu*, literally "beautiful potato-moon."

On the thirteenth of the ninth month (October in the solar calendar) offerings are again made in admiration of the full moon. This is the Thirteenth Night. The most popular offerings are **chestnuts**, so it is also known as the *kurimeigetsu*, or "beautiful chestnut moon." In the past, viewing only one or the other full moons of the Fifteenth and Thirteenth Nights was known as *katamitsuki*, or single moon viewing, and **was frowned upon**.

「十五夜」と「十三夜」の違い

旧暦の秋は7〜9月。そのど真ん中である8月15日に出るのが中秋の月（十五夜）。この月を観賞する行事が「お月見」であるが、「お花見」と違って酒宴とは結びつかない。日本は、**ススキ**の穂や月見団子、サトイモ、枝豆などを飾る程度。収穫祭でもあったから別名「芋名月」。

翌月の9月13日にもやはり月への供え物をし、月を愛でる。これが「十三夜」。供え物の主役が**栗**になったりするので別名「栗名月」。かつては、この「十五夜」と「十三夜」の両方を見ないで片方だけ見るのを、「片見月」と呼んで**嫌った**。

9 *Omatsuri*: Festivals
お祭り

In spring to pray for a good harvest, in fall to give thanks for the harvest

Until the Edo period taxes and salaries were paid in agricultural and marine produce, such as rice and fish, so **crop yields** and **fish catches** were a matter of life or death. People were powerless against insect damage and weather variability, and so all they could do was to pray and make offerings to the gods and Buddha in early spring before the start of the farming and fishing seasons. And then, if they achieved bumper crops and catches as hoped for, they would offer thanks to the gods and Buddha. These events held in villages are the spring and summer festivals, and their origins must have been similar the world over.

When several good years follow in succession, people become better off and the festivals become more **elaborate**. They dress in matching *yukata* and *happi* coats, carry the *mikoshi* shrine, play festival music with gongs, drums, and flutes, and festival floats carry singers and dancers. **Paper lanterns** are lit, **stalls** are set up, people join in the circle of dancers, and the night sky is lit up by **fireworks** set off from the waters edge…

豊作を祈る春、豊作を感謝する秋

税や給与が米や魚などの農林水産物で支払われていた江戸時代までの日本では、毎年の**作物のでき具合**や**漁の水揚げ高**が死活問題だった。虫の害や気候変動にも無力だった。そのため農作業や漁を始める春先には神仏に祈り、供物を出して祀るしかなかった。そして期待通りの豊作や豊漁があれば、その神仏に感謝を捧げた。集落単位のこの行事が春や秋の祭りであり、その起源は世界中で似たようなものだったはずだ。

幸運な年が続けばゆとりが生まれ、祭りにも**彩りが加わる**。そろいの浴衣や法被を身に着け、神輿をかつぎ、鉦や太鼓や笛のお囃子が付き、引き回される山車には歌い手や踊り手が乗せられた。**提灯**がゆらめき、**屋台店**が並び、人々が踊りの輪に加わり、水辺から**花火**が打ち上げられて夜空に大輪の火の華をひらいた……。

10 Ōmisoka: New Year's Eve
大晦日

The very last night of the year

Misoka, literally "thirtieth day," refers to the end of the month, and this is prefixed with *ō*, meaning "great," to indicate the last day of the twelfth month—that is, the very last day of the year. Another word for this is *ō-tsugomori*, *tsugomori* meaning literally "hidden moon" and also refers to the last day of the month—or of the year, when prefixed with *ō*.

How people spend this evening was determined in the 1950s when, on New Year's Eve in 1953, the public broadcaster NHK decided to televise the Red vs. White Kōhaku Singing Contest (in which women singers are Red and men singers are White) that had hitherto been broadcast on radio in the New Year. It was a huge hit, attracting 81.4% of the **viewing ratings** in 1963. Even now, sixty years later, it still gets around 40% of the ratings. Therefore most families spend the evening watching this program. So first of all, families watch this program on TV. Dinner is *soba* noodles. *Soba*, or buckwheat, is grown all over Japan, but it is thought that the method of kneading the flour into dough then cutting it into noodles started in the sixteenth century. In a corny Edo-style pun, the long, thin noodles are said to represent the desire to live a long and frugal life. They were apparently eaten on New Year's Day during the Edo period.

１年の最後の夜の過ごし方

「おおみそか」の「みそか(晦日)」というのは「三十日」つまり月末のことであり、12月の月末は1年の最後の日なので「大みそか」または「大つごもり」という。「つごもり」は「月が出なくなる」＝「月隠り」からきている。

　この夜の過ごし方は、1950年代に決まった。公共放送NHKがそれまで正月になってからラジオでやっていた男女＝紅白対抗（女性が紅組、男性が白組）の歌合戦を1953年の大みそかにテレビでも放送することにしたからだ。これが人気を呼び、1963年には**視聴率**81.4%を打

Chapter 1 Annual Events

ち出した。以来60年経っても40%前後の高視聴率を維持している。だから、まず家庭のTVではこの番組が流れている。そして夜食に出されるのが「そば」である。そばの実は世界各地で使われている食材だが、粉を練ってから切って麺状にする「そば切り」は、日本では16世紀頃に生まれた食べ方とされる。「細く長く生きられますように」という江戸風のダジャレだ。その江戸時代には元旦に食べたともいわれる。

Ringing out the old year, and *ni-nen mairi*

Another word for New Year's Eve is *joya*, which means removing all the misfortunes of the year. In major temples, the temple bell is rung 108 times. This represents the number of earthly desires, such as **greed**, **avarice**, and **lust**, that people have.

Whether ringing the bell is completed within the old year, **straddles the year**, or wholly in the New Year varies according to the temple. Also, when the *hatsumōde*, or first shrine visit of the New Year, is started on New Year's Eve and continues into the New Year, it is called *ni-nen mairi*, or "two-year visit" (to see out the old year, and welcome the new year).

除夜の鐘と「2年参り」

　大みそかの夜は別名「除夜」ともいう。1年の間に重なった厄災を除

くという意味だ。大きな寺では鐘楼の鐘を108回打ち鳴らす。108というのは人間が持つ**食欲・金銭欲・色欲**などの煩悩の数とされる。この108回を年内につき終えるか、**年をまたぐか**、新年になってからつくかは寺によって異なる。また、普通は年が明けてから行う「初詣で」を、大みそかの夜から来てお参りするのを「2年参り」という。

第 2 章
Chapter 2

人生
Life Events

出　産	❶	Birth
七五三	❷	*Shichi-go-san*: Childhood Milestones
成　人	❸	Coming of Age
賀　寿	❹	Long-life Celebrations
厄　年	❺	*Yakudoshi*: Unlucky Years

1 Birth
出産

What women do in the fifth month of pregnancy

In the Kakigarachō district of Nihonbashi in Tokyo, there is a shrine called Suitengū. It is a branch of the main temple in Kurume, Kyushu, and is dedicated to protecting children and to water, but two or three times a month on the Day of the Dog, it is crowded with young women visiting the shrine accompanied by their parents and husbands. They all have the same **objectives**: "Please let me be blessed with children," "Please give me an easy delivery," or "Thank you for letting me give birth safely." The reason the shrine is particularly busy on the Day of the Dog is that the dog is believed to give birth many times without problems. Women come here to have **prayers** said for **safe delivery** and to purchase *iwata-obi* maternity bands.

妊娠5ヵ月目に妊婦がすること

東京・日本橋蛎殻町に水天宮という神社がある。九州の久留米市に本宮があって子供と水の守り神とされるが、月に2、3度ある「戌の日」となると、若い女性とその親や夫らしき人との参拝客で大変な賑わいになる。参拝客の**目的**は同じで、「子供を授かりたい」「安産でありたい」あるいは「無事に出産できたことを感謝したい」というもの。「戌の日」がとくに混雑するのは、犬が安産・多産だと信じられているからだ。女性たちはここに来て**安産**の**祈禱**をしてもらったり、「岩田帯」を買い求めたりする。

Are 100-day-old babies fed stones?

In the past, pregnancy and childbirth were considered unclean. The truth is, though, that this meant they were handled sensitively and special attention paid to the health and cleanliness of the mother and her newborn baby. This is also evident in the various events held following the birth. For example, the seventh night after birth is called *oshichiya*, and is when a naming ceremony is held for the baby. Legally, the birth should be registered within fourteen days, but more than a few couples hold this ceremony together with their parents. Also, about a month after birth, a shrine visit is made to inform the local **deity** of the child's birth. And on the 100th day, a weaning ceremony is held, for which a feast is prepared and prayers given that the child will never lack for food. A unique feature of this is a small stone or stones placed on the dining table as a **talisman** for the baby to grow strong, healthy teeth.

生後100日目の乳児に石を食べさせる？

かつて妊娠・出産は穢れ多きものと見なされた。でも本当は、そうして特別に慎重に対処することで母体と新生児が清潔・健康に過ごせるようにと願ったからだといわれる。それは誕生後の様々な行事があることからもうかがえる。たとえば生まれて7日目夜は「お七夜」といい、赤ちゃんに命名する儀式がある。法律的には出産後14日以内に役所に届ければ良いのだが、両親を含めてこの儀式を行う夫婦は少なくない。また、ほぼひと月たつと、子供の誕生を近所の**氏神様**に報告する「お宮参り」がある。そして100日目には「お食い初め」の儀式があり、ご馳走を用意し、子供が一生、食べるもので困らないようにと願う。ユニークなのは、食膳に小さな石が添えてあることで、やがて生えそろう歯が石のように丈夫でありますようにという**まじない**である。

2 *Shichi-go-san*: Childhood Milestones
七五三

Relief when the child reaches the age of seven in good health

Even if a child survives **infancy**, the worries of parents do not end there. Indeed, an infant's development was considered so risky that there's a saying "Children are in the hands of the gods until the age of seven." In Japan it became popular to hold ceremonies at the ages of three, five, and seven to pray for the safe growth of a child, a practice known as *shichi-go-san* (7–5–3). There are variations in different regions, but on or around November 15, girls aged three or seven, and boys aged three or five are dressed up and go with their parents to visit a shrine or temple. There they buy long sticks of red and white candy called *chitose-ame* (1,000-year candy), which is considered lucky and said to enable them to live for a thousand years.

7歳まで無事に育てばひと安心

こうして**乳児期**を無事に乗り切っても、まだまだ安心はできないのが親心。何しろ「7つ前は神のうち」という言葉があるくらい、乳幼児の成育は神様しだいと思われていた。そこで日本では3歳、5歳、7歳と奇数年齢を目安にして、神仏に無事な成長を祈る「七五三」の儀式が普及した。地方によって違いはあるものの、女の子は3歳と7歳、男の子は3歳と5歳になった年の11月15日前後に、盛装して両親とともに近所の神社や寺にお参りをする。そこで、縁起が良いとされる「千歳飴」を買ったりもする。なにせこの紅白模様の細長い飴を食べると1000歳まで長生きできるのだ。

3 Coming of Age
成人

Ceremony at which children are recognized as independent adults

Any parent, having successfully raised their child, will next hope to see them able to stand on their own feet as an adult. The Coming-of-Age ceremony held when they reach the age at which society considers them adult is a grand and solemn occasion filled with thanks as well as blessings and hopes for the future. In the past, when the **average life expectancy** in Japan was age forty (which was actually the case up to 1920), a *kakanshiki* (crowning ceremony, to fit boys with a traditional cap) or *genpukushiki* (coming-of-age ceremony) was held for boys aged around fifteen years, while the *jūsan iwai* (thirteen celebration) was held for girls around age thirteen. By going through these ceremonies, children joined the ranks of adults, and a samurai coming of age would receive his own stipend (salary) the following year. These days, local governments hold a coming-of-age ceremony on the second Monday in January for all those who turned twenty during the past year. Some regions hold it to coincide with the Obon week in summer when people go back to their home towns.

自立した大人として認められる儀式

　子供が無事に育てば、次は「大人として独り立ちできるように」と願うのも当然の親心。そして社会的に一人前と見なされる年齢に達したとき、感謝と将来へ祝福や期待を込めて盛大かつ厳粛に行うのが成人の儀式である。**平均寿命**が40歳台だった昔の日本（といっても1920年代まで続いた）では、男の子が15歳前後になると冠を着ける「加冠式」あるいは「元服式」を行い、女の子は13歳前後で「十三祝い」を行った。この儀式を経ることで外見的にも大人の仲間入りをし、侍で成人した場合は翌年から一人前の「扶持（給与）」をもらえた。現代の日本では20歳を迎えた年度の1月第2月曜に地方自治体などが「成人式」を催す。帰省しやすい夏のお盆に行う地方もある。

Chapter 2 Life Events

Long-life Celebrations
賀寿(がじゅ)

Age 60: *Kanreki* and wearing an *akachanchanko* red padded vest

As may be deduced from the above explanation, if you somehow survive until your sixty-first year, your birth year animal will be repeated, and this longevity is something to be celebrated. Why, then, are you expected to celebrate such an auspicious occasion by wearing a red headscarf or **padded vest** and sitting on a red cushion? One theory is that by completing the sixty-year cycle (the literal meaning of *kanreki*) and returning to your birth year, you are returning to being a baby, which gives rise to some witty word play. The word for baby in Japanese is 赤ちゃん *akachan*, where 赤 means "red," and ちゃん doubled gives you *chanchan*, the beginning of the word *chanchanko* which is a Japanese-style padded vest. Another theory holds that according to **feng shui**, red is a strong color that protects against evil. Confucius called the age of sixty "obedient ears" since at that age you should be able to **take other people's opinion in your stride**—in other words, complaining that wearing red is a vulgar custom of unknown origins is really beneath you at that age.

「赤いちゃんちゃんこ」を着る還暦(かんれき)

　以上の説明で察しがつくと思うが、人生を何とか生き抜いて、自分の生まれた年が数え年61歳で巡ってくるというのは、祝うべき長寿（賀寿）ということになる。それは良いとしても、なぜその祝いに赤い頭巾、赤い**ちゃんちゃんこ**を着て、赤い座布団に座らされるのかがわかりにくい。暦がひと巡りすることは生まれた赤ん坊に戻ること（本卦(ほんけ)還り）だという考え方はある。そこで「赤ちゃん＝赤ちゃんちゃんこ」と洒落たのだという説がある。また赤色は、**風水**的に魔よけの強い色だからとの説もある。孔子は、この年齢くらいになったら**他人の意見に従え**という意味で60歳を「耳順(じじゅん)」と呼んだ。赤づくしなんて由来の知れぬ悪趣味だと怒るのは大人気ないらしい。

Chapter 2 Life Events

5 *Yakudoshi:* Unlucky Years
厄年

The ages 42 for men and 33 for women require caution

Adding on the years is not always something to be celebrated. There are also danger years that are said to be potentially **calamitous**, called *yakudoshi*, or unlucky years. The main ones that everyone knows about are the ages 42 for men and 33 for women (both in the traditional Japanese way of calculating age), but there are also the moderately unlucky years of 25 and 61 for men (*kanreki* is also an unlucky year for them!), and 19 and 37 for women. The years before and after a *yakudoshi* also require **vigilance**. Those approaching a *yakudoshi* should visit a temple or shrine to ward off the misfortune, take care of their physical health, and **act prudently**. It is not only the person himself who is affected, but the calamity may **befall** his whole family.

男42歳、女33歳は要注意の年齢

年齢を重ねることはめでたいとは限らない。人生には**災厄が待ち構えている**危険な年齢もあるというのが「厄年」である。一般に知られているのは、男42歳、女33歳（いずれも数え年）の「大厄」で、中程度だと男25と61歳（還暦も厄年！）、女19歳と37歳がそれに当たる。そしてこれらの厄年の1年前は「前厄」、1年後は「後厄」と呼んでやはり**注意**を要する年齢ということになっている。そして「厄年」を迎える人は寺社でお払い（厄除け）をしてもらい、体調を気遣い、**行動を自重する**べきだとされる。やっかいなのは当人だけでなく、その家族にも災厄が**及ぶ**ことがあるという。

Chapter 2 Life Events

第3章
Chapter 3

婚礼 / 葬儀 / 宗教
Weddings, Funerals, and Religions

婚　　約 ❶ Engagement
結婚式と披露宴 ❷ The Wedding Ceremony and Reception
式日 / 六曜 ❸ Auspicious and Unlucky Days
葬　　儀 ❹ Funerals
神と仏 ❺ Gods and the Buddha
民間信仰 ❻ Folk Beliefs

1 Engagement
婚約

An engagement sealed by dried bonito, dried squid, and kelp?

Ceremonies to seal an engagement ahead of marriage are held in many countries. In Japan, the go-between, the groom and his parents proceed to the bride's home with money in an envelope marked *obiryō* (**betrothal money**) and other gifts to mark the occasion. This ceremonial exchange of betrothal gifts, called *yuinōkin* (money) and *yuinōhin* (other items), marks the joining together of the two families. This betrothal money is sometimes given as a **dowry** on the occasion of the marriage.

What is particularly Japanese about the betrothal gifts are the items given. These are all based on auspicious wordplay. For example, **dried bonito** is *katsuo-bushi*, a homophone for 勝つ男, indicating the man's dependability; **dried squid** is *surume*, a homophone for 寿留女, indicating a wish for many years of happiness for the woman; and **kelp** is *konbu*, a homophone for 子生婦, indicating a desire for **numerous offspring**; and an open fan indicates a desire for increasing prosperity over the years. However, the details differ between eastern and western Japan.

「婚約」に鰹節やスルメや昆布？

結婚に先立って「婚約」の儀式をする習慣は多くの国にある。日本では、新婦の家に仲人と新郎とその両親が出向いて、「帯料」と書いたお金と記念の品々を贈る。両方の家が結ばれることを了承するこの儀式を「結納」、贈られるお金は「結納金」、品々は「結納品」と呼ぶ。この「結納金」は新婦が嫁入りの際に「持参金」とする場合もある。

日本的なのは「結納品」の品々である。すべて縁起の良い語呂合わせで組み合わされる。たとえば**鰹節**は「勝つ男」で男性の頼もしさを、長期保存できる**スルメ**は「寿留女」で末永い幸せを、**昆布**は「子生婦」で**子孫繁栄**を、扇は開いた形から「末広がり」の繁栄を…といった具合。ただし関東と関西では内容が違うものもある。

The Wedding Ceremony and Reception
結婚式と披露宴

Sansankudo: exchanging nuptial cups

Wedding ceremonies were not held in Japan until the Middle Ages. The norm was for men to visit their wives' homes in "commuter marriages," and at the appropriate time a reception was held to inform everyone of this. From the Edo period until the mid-twentieth century (prewar), the norm was for the families and relatives of both sides to be invited to the groom's home for a banquet prepared by local housewives. The wedding **oath** was a simple ritual known as *sansankudo*, in which a stack of three sake cups of different sizes were filled three times (a total of nine cups), each shared by the couple.

「三々九度」の盃を交わすだけの誓い

　中世までの日本では結婚式はなかった。男性が女性のところに通う「通い婚」が普通であり、周囲にそのことを知らせる適当な時期に「披露宴」を行っていた。江戸時代から20世紀半ば（戦前）までは、新郎の家で双方の家族やゆかりのある人などを招き、近所の主婦などが世話して宴を設ける「人前式」が普通だった。結婚の**誓い**も、新郎新婦が大小3組の酒盃をそれぞれ3回にわけて（合計9回）飲む「三々九度」の儀式だけだった。

A variety of wedding ceremonies

These days there are many different types of weddings held in Japan. In addition to non-religious ceremonies, there are also Shinto weddings, Buddhist weddings, and Christian weddings. Shinto weddings are said to have their roots in the marriage of Emperor Taisho in 1900, and Christian ceremonies in that of Joseph Hardy Neesima to his wife Yae. According to a survey by the wedding magazine *Zexy* (2009), 99% of couples didn't use a go-between, 60.4% had a Christian ceremony (in second place was a secular ceremony at 20.4%, and a Shinto ceremony in third place at 17%). Incidentally, there are fewer than three million Christians in Japan, but many people think it's cool to hold a Christian-style ceremony.

多様化した結婚式

　現代の日本の結婚式は多様である。「人前式」以外にも「神前式」、「仏前式」、「キリスト教式」などがある。「神前式」のルーツは1900年の大正天皇の結婚式、「キリスト教式」のルーツは1876年の新島襄・八重の結婚式といわれる。結婚雑誌「ゼクシィ」の調査（2009年）によると、カップルの99％は仲人を立てず、60.4％がキリスト教式（2位は人前式20.4％、3位神前式17％）だった。ちなみに日本のキリスト教信者は300万人に過ぎないが、キリスト教式の挙式がカッコイイと考える人が多いのだ。

O-ironaoshi and *hikidemono*

It was only since the period of rapid economic growth in the 1960s that the wedding reception became a **showy affair**. The most Japanese elements of the proceedings are probably the *o-ironaoshi,* the bride's change of outfit, and *hikidemono*, the gifts given to guests to take home with them. Originally, the bride would change from the all-white kimono and elaborate bridal robe worn for the ceremony into a relatively simple but colored kimono to indicate her eagerness to get to work in the marital home. However, at some point this became a show of changing from a Western-style wedding dress into a **sumptuous** kimono (or sometimes the other way round), and even the bridegrooms have got in on the act now. The *hikidemono* has its roots in celebrations held by court nobles during the Heian period, when a horse would be brought out into the garden and presented to the **guest of honor**. Nowadays this has become an item of food or crockery given to guests as a **memento**, and sometimes even a catalogue from which guests can choose their own gift.

「お色直し」と「引き出物」

　披露宴が**華やかなもの**になるのは1960年代の高度成長期からである。その演出の中で日本的なのは「お色直し」と「引き出物」かもしれない。「お色直し」は、本来、花嫁が礼服である白無垢や打掛けから、色のついた比較的地味な着物に着替え、少しでも早く嫁いだ家で働くことを示すものだった。しかしいつの間にかウェディングドレスから**豪華な**着物（あるいはその逆）に着替えて見せるショーになり、花婿まで「お色直し」するようになってきた。また「引き出物」は、平安時代に貴族が祝い事の際に馬を庭先に引き出して**賓客**に贈呈したのがルーツだった。それが現代になって食器セットなどの**記念品**を参加者に贈呈するものになり、さらには自由なものを選べるカタログ方式になっている。

③ Auspicious and Unlucky Days
式日／六曜

Good and bad days to hold an event

The days on which important ceremonies should be held, whether **felicitous occasions** such as weddings or **unfortunate occasions** such as funerals, are called *shikijitsu*. These are determined by the cycle of six lucky and unlucky days known as *rokuyō*. It's not clear whether or not this is originally from the Chinese doctrine of yin yang, but in one month there are thought to be five cycles of six days which determined how to proceed with, say, a war, or a ceremony. Also, each of these days has its own particular meaning, which is why it is said, for example, that weddings should be held on *taian* days, and that funerals should not be held on *tomobiki* days.

何かを行うのに良い日、悪い日

婚礼やなどの**慶事**や葬式などの**弔事**など、重要な儀式を行う日を式日という。その際に目安になるのが、「先勝」「友引」「大安」「仏滅」などその日ごとに替わる六種類の「六曜」である。元は中国の陰陽道だというがはっきりしないが1ヵ月を5週間×6日とし、その時の星回りから戦争や儀式の進め方を決めた。そして「結婚式は大安に」、「葬式は友引を避ける」などといわれるようになったのは、六曜ごとに意味があるからだ。

Senshō (or **sakigachi**): whatever you do, better do it early. The morning is lucky, afternoon unlucky.

Tomobiki: a day when your luck affects other people, so should be avoided for unfortunate occasions. In the case of competitive events, the result will be a draw.

Senbu (or **sakimake**): haste will end in failure. Mornings are unlucky, afternoons lucky.

Butsumetsu: the day of Buddha's death, the unluckiest day. Celebrations and competitive events should be avoided.

Taian (or **daian**): the luckiest day, although good luck can easily change to bad luck, so care is needed.

Shakkō (or **sekiguchi**): an unlucky day, although the two hours around noon are lucky. Beware of fire and blood.

先勝（せんしょう・さきがち）：何事も先んじた方が良い。午前中が吉で午後が凶

友引（ともびき）：友を引き込むことから凶事は避ける。勝負事なら引き分けになる。

先負（せんぶ・さきまけ）：急ぐと失敗する。午前中は凶で午後からが吉。

仏滅（ぶつめつ）：仏が滅した大凶の日。祝い事や勝負事は避ける。

大安（たいあん・だいあん）：最高に吉の日。ただしすぐ凶に転じやすいので要注意。

赤口（しゃっこう・せきぐち）:凶の日だが正午前後2時間は吉。火や血に注意。

4 Funerals
葬儀

Why the vast majority of funerals are Buddhist

Births and deaths are occasions that put people in a **solemn** frame of mind. There are various types of funeral services around the world, but in Japan the Buddhist service has been the most common since the Edo period. This is because there was a strictly enforced system to ensure that everyone in the community (parishioners) was registered to a Buddhist temple, regardless of sect. The temples were effectively community managers, overseeing coming-of-age, marriage, burial, and other ceremonial occasions as well as the **family registers**, so they also came to serve as a mutual aid organization for farm work. Even now, when that system no longer exists, many people hold a Buddhist service for funerals.

仏教式が圧倒的に多い理由

人の誕生と死は、人の心を**厳粛**にする。世界各地にはさまざまな弔いの儀式があるが、日本では江戸時代以降、仏教式で行われることが多い。これは、集落の住民（信徒）を各宗派の寺（檀家寺）に管理させる「寺請制度」が徹底されたからだ。寺が共同体の冠婚葬祭行事の執行役と**戸籍係**を兼ねたようなもので、農作業などでの相互扶助の仕組みとも一体になっていた。制度がなくなった現代でも葬儀は仏教式で行われることが多い。

Memorial services held after death

A number of services are held following a death. Buddhist services for mourning, called *hōyō*, are held at certain intervals over time. The seventh day after death is *shonanuka*, and every seventh day after that is also observed until the main turning point at the forty-ninth day (7 x 7 days). This is the point at which the deceased's soul goes to the **Pure Land** where Buddha resides. The ashes are interred and the **memorial tablet** is placed on the family altar. After this, other specified dates are the hundredth day, the one-year anniversary, the second anniversary, the sixth anniversary, the twelfth anniversary, the thirty-second anniversary, and so on. On these major dates, a priest chants sutras, and the **bereaved family** and relatives **visit the grave** and have dinner together.

死後の仏事（法事）

葬礼は死後も続く。追悼のために「法要」とよばれる仏教儀式が月日の区切りごとに行われる。死んで7日目が「初七日」で、以後7日ごとに行われるが大きな節目は「四十九日（7×7日目）」。この日を境に死者の霊魂が仏の住む**浄土**に行く。墓への納骨や**位牌**を仏壇に納める。以後は、「百か日」「一周忌（1年目）」「三回忌」「七回忌」「十三回忌」「三十三回忌」などと続く。大きな法要のときは僧侶による読経、**墓参**、**遺族**・親族による会食などを行う。

Chapter 3 Weddings, Funerals, and Religions

5 Gods and the Buddha
神と仏

A country where the gods and the Buddha have always coexisted

It is said that Japanese people are not particularly religious. It's true that we take newborn babies to a Shinto shrine to be blessed, hold Christian weddings, and Buddhist funerals. At New Year we pray to our *kamidana* (Shinto home shrine) and at Obon to our *butsudan* (Buddhist home altar), and we buy sweets for Valentine's and Christmas. It's not that we don't believe in religion at all, but rather that we pick-and-mix the way we use them.

Even in the **precincts** of a shrine or temple there may be an *inari* fox deity or a *tenjinsama* god, which many foreigners who have grown up under a strict **monotheistic religion** find hard to understand.

今も昔も神と仏が混在する国

　日本人は宗教的に厳格でないといわれる。たしかに生まれた時は神社に「お宮参り」に行き、結婚式はキリスト教式で行い、死んだら仏教で弔う。お正月には神棚に向かい、お盆には仏壇に手を合わせ、バレンタインやクリスマスにはスイーツを買い求める。宗教を信じない無宗教ではなく、つごうに合わせて使い分けている。

　神社や寺院にしても、**敷地**の一角に「なんとか稲荷」や「天神様」などがあったりするのだから、厳格な**一神教**の文化で育った外国人にはわかりにくい。

History of the rivalry and coexistence of Shinto and Buddhism

Buddhism particularly became very powerful, and the theory that Shinto gods are the earthly manifestations of the heavenly buddhas and bodhissatvas became mainstream. Amaterasu became Dainichi Nyorai, while Hachiman, as who Emperor Ōjin was deified, was assimilated as Hachiman Great Bodhissatva (a bodhissatva is a trainee Buddha).

This underwent another big change in the **Meiji Restoration**, the objective of which was to restore to power the imperial line that boasted an unbroken connection to Emperor Jinmu, who was descended from Amaterasu. This was effectively a **theocracy**. Buddhism was seen as a foreign import and should be abolished, and there was the *haibutsu kishaku* movement to destroy Buddhist temples and statues. The drive to banish Buddhism and revive Shinto continued until the end of the Pacific War. Shinto ceased to be the state religion with the **emperor's public renunciation of divinity** and the occupation's Shinto Directive designed to effect the separation of state and religion.

神道と仏教の競合と混在の歴史

なかでも仏教は大きな力を持つようになり、「日本の神々は、仏教の仏が仮の姿をとったもの」だとする説「本地垂迹説」が主流になった。アマテラスは「大日如来」の化身、応神天皇を祀る八幡様は「八幡大菩薩」(菩薩は仏をめざす修行者)といった具合で、神道支持勢力が取り込まれた。これがもう一度大きく変わるのは**明治維新**である。

維新の旗印は、アマテラスから神武天皇につながる血脈を誇る天皇による親政が再開された「王政復古」にある。**神政一致**だ。外来の仏教は廃すべきとなり、寺院や仏像を破棄する「廃仏毀釈」運動も起きた。仏教軽視、神道復活の流れは太平洋戦争終了まで続いた。戦後は**天皇の人間宣言**と占領軍の神道指令、政教分離政策で、国家神道は終わりとなる。

Clap your hands at shrines, and bring your hands together at temples

The custom of Japanese people to differentiate the way of practising Shinto and Buddhism can also be seen in the different ways of praying at shrines and temples. First, the etiquette at shrines. As you pass through the *torii*, you will see a **water trough** to one side where you can cleanse your hands. Then, standing before the shrine, shake the rope hanging from the large bell hanging from a beam to summon the *kami*. Stand up straight and throw some change into the offertory box, then perform the bowing and clapping ritual: bow twice, clap your hands twice, then bow once more (the sequence may vary according to the shrine). This type of clapping is called *kashiwade*. At a funeral, or after an accident or disaster, you should not make any sound as you clap. On the other hand, when praying at a temple you simply bring your hands together in silence to express your thanks.

神社では手を打ち、寺では手を合わせる

　　神仏を使い分ける日本人の習慣は、神社と寺での祈り方の違いに出る。まず神社での作法。鳥居をくぐると参道の脇に「手水（ちょうず）」場がある。ここで口と手を清めたら、神殿の前に立ち、梁にかかった大きな鈴から垂れる綱を揺すって神様を呼ぶ。姿勢を正して小銭の「賽銭（さいせん）」を入れたら「二礼二拍手一礼」を行う。2度お辞儀をし、2度手を打ちならし、最後にもう一度お辞儀をするのである（神社によって回数が違ったりする）。この拍手を「かしわ手」という。なお、葬礼など凶事の際は、手を打っても音を出さないようにするとの決まりもある。一方、寺での祈りは静かに両手を合わせるだけで、感謝の気持ちを表している。

6 Folk Beliefs
民間信仰

Tenjin, Benten, and Inari

It is often difficult to discern whether a sacred site in Japan is Buddhist or Shinto, and many are simply dedicated to a desire to gain material benefit through prayer. For example, Tenjin was originally a god that governed the weather. However, after the death in exile of the scholar and politican Sugawara no Michizane (845–903), who had been falsely accused and banished to Kyushu, many **important personages** there met a violent death in natural disasters rumored to be the result of Michizane's **curse.** The shocked court subsequently **deified** him as Tenjin, who thenceforth became known throughout the land as the god of scholarship and children, and even now students taking exams visit Tenjin shrines. Benten, also known as Benzaiten, is one of the deities that protects Shakyamuni, but in Japan she is also the goddess of wealth and of the arts, particularly music, so is worshiped by geisha and other workers in the nightlife business. Inari was worshipped long ago by the powerful Hata clan, and became known as the god of rice and bountiful harvests, and later as the god of good business, so more and more people made offerings of numerous small red *torii* and white fox messengers. Sometimes offerings of deep-fried tofu, which foxes are known to like, can also be seen.

天神様、弁天様、お稲荷様

　神様なのか仏様なのか区別がつきにくい聖地がたくさんあるのも日本の特徴で、多くは庶民の現世利益を願う素朴な信仰対象である。たとえば「天神様」は、もともと天候を支配する神だったが、学者であり政治家でもあった菅原道真（845-903）が讒訴によって九州

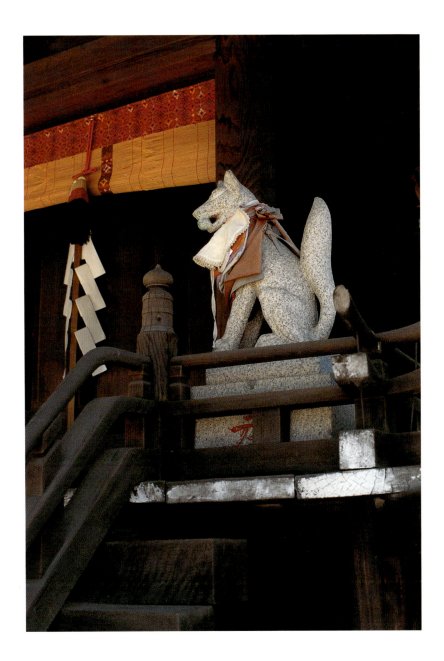

に左遷された。その死後、天変地異が起こり、**要人**が変死するなどして「道真のたたり」と噂された。これに驚いた朝廷は彼を天神として祀ったのが起源であり、以後、学問の神様、子供の神様として全国に広まり、今も受験生がお参りしている。また、「弁天様」こと「弁財天」は、お釈迦様を守る神のひとりだが、日本では蓄財と技芸とくに音楽の神様とされ、芸者さんや水商売に従事する人の信仰を集めている。「お稲荷様」は大昔の豪族である秦氏の家で祀られたものだが、稲つまり豊穣を叶える神様として広まり、それが商売繁盛の神になり、たくさんの小さな赤い鳥居と神の使いである白い狐を奉納する人が増えた。狐の好物として油揚げを供えている光景も見かける。

Chapter 3

Weddings, Funerals, and Religions

The Seven Lucky Gods

Japanese people generally feel that lots of gods are luckier than one, and the *shichifukujin,* or seven lucky gods are unique to Japan. They include Daikokuten, Bishamonten, Benzaiten, Hotei, Fukurokuju, Jurōjin, and Ebisu, and grant the kind of wishes that appeal to ordinary people, such as bountiful harvests, long life, wealth, and beauty. Other than Ebisu, the god of fishermen, they are a multinational group originating in, amongst others, Hinduism and Taoism. And if these Seven Lucky Gods in their treasure ship laden with gold, silver, **coral** and other precious items, appear in your dreams on January 1, it is said your wishes will be granted. Also, at New Year quite a few people tour several locations where these gods are enshrined.

おめでたいのは「七福神」

　神様は1人よりたくさんの方がありがたい気持ちがするのは庶民の心。福をもたらす7人の神を集めたのが日本独特の「七福神」。メンバーは、「大黒天」「毘沙門天」「弁財天」「布袋」「福禄寿」「寿老人」「恵比寿」で豊作、長生き、金持ち、美人にという庶民的な願いを叶えてくれる神様たち。豊漁の神「恵比寿」以外は、ヒンドゥー教や道教などに起源をもつ多国籍軍団でもある。そしてこの七福神が、金銀や**サンゴ**などの宝物を満載して乗ってくるのが「宝船」で、元旦の夜にこの夢を見ると、夢が叶うといわれた。また、正月には、いろいろな場所に祀られているこれらの神様をお参りする「七福神めぐり」のツアーに出かける人も少なくない。

Lord Enma, the bane of liars!

Gods do not only listen to your mundane wishes. Enma Daio appears in the popular manga *Dragon Ball* as King Yemma, the fearsome judge of hell who punishes people according to the sins they committed when alive. He easily sees through anyone who lies in order to escape, and that's why in the past adults threatened children with, "If you lie, Lord Enma will pull out your tongue!" On the other hand, there are times when you want to borrow his miraculous power and so people also pray to him in earnest. Incidentally, his favorite food is said to be *konnyaku*, or devil's tongue jelly.

ウソをつくと怖い「えんま様」

俗世間の願い事だけをきく神様ばかりではない。人気アニメ『ドラゴンボール』にも登場する「閻魔大王」は、地獄の裁判官であり、死者の生前の**罪**を裁いて罰を与えるおそろしい存在だ。その場のがれのウソをついても簡単に見破られてしまう。だから昔の子供たちは、「ウソをつくと、えんま様に舌を抜かれるぞ」と大人たちに脅かされたものである。反面、その強面の霊力を借りたいときもある。だからこの神様に祈るときは**真剣**だ。ちなみに好物は**こんにゃく**だとされる。

Jizō: god of children and local community

Jizō, who really looks like a small child with a shaved head, is worshipped all over Japan. There are various theories about his religious status, but at the end of the day he is the deity who appears in child form in hell and on earth to save us from **epidemics**, **starvation**, and other sufferings. People also pray to him for the healthy growth of children, and to comfort the souls of children who had the misfortune of dying young. In Kyoto and some other places, there is a Jizō Festival during Obon when people gather before the local Jizō hall to pray, and the adults pass around sweets.

子供と地域の神様「お地蔵さん」

頭をそった小さな子供のような表情の「地蔵」は、日本中のいたるところに祀られている。信仰上の位置づけは諸説あるのだが、要するに地獄でも現世でも子供の姿でやってきてくれて**疫病**や**飢餓**などの苦難から救ってくれるのがこの神様。子供の健やかな成長を祈ったり、不幸にして早く死んだ子供の霊を慰めるために祀られることもある。京都などでは、お盆の時期に近所の地蔵堂の前に集まって祈り、大人たちからお菓子をふるまわれたりする「地蔵盆」という行事がある。

Worshipping Mt. Fuji

In June 2013, UNESCO approved Mount Fuji as a **World Heritage** site. The reason it is not considered a natural heritage despite being a mountain is that it has clearly been an important element in Japanese culture as an object of faith for Japanese people since ancient times, well-represented in art including *waka* poems and *ukiyoe* woodblock prints. Mountain worship has been practiced all over the country since antiquity, but Mount Fuji is said to have become a particular object of worship during the Edo period. Clubs were formed in Edo and the surrounding areas to visit Sengen Shrines worshipping Mount Fuji, with the climb to witness sunrise at the peak considered the highlight of the year.

富士山信仰

　2013年6月、ユネスコは富士山を**世界文化遺産**として認定した。山なのに自然遺産でないのは、この山が古くから日本人の信仰の対象として神聖視され、また和歌や浮世絵などの題材ともなって、日本文化の重要な構成要素だったと認定したからだ。山岳信仰は古くから各地にあるが、富士山信仰が盛んになったのは江戸時代半ばからといわれる。富士をご神体とする浅間神社に詣でるために、庶民たちが仲間（講）を集める「富士講」が江戸と周辺各地に生まれ、頂上に上って日の出を仰ぐ「ご来光」がイベントのハイライトとみなされるようになった。

Omikuji: fortune telling by the gods

After dinner at a Chinese restaurant in the United States, diners are given a fortune cookie. People in the West and East both like fortune telling. In Japan, slips of paper telling your fortune, called *omikuji,* are sold at shrines and temples. There are various different types of *omikuji*, but the most common are those that grade fortunes from *daikichi* (excellent) to *daikyō* (terrible), with sections on health, love, finances, competitions, and so forth. If you get a good fortune, while being happy about it you should beware of being too elated, and if it's a bad fortune you should think positively that it's a sign that things will be better next time. After reading the fortune, you should tie it to the fence or tree provided rather than take it home with you. This signifies sealing your fate with the gods. Incidentally, 70% of these fortune slips are made by a company called Joshidōsha based in Shūnan City in Yamaguchi prefecture.

「おみくじ」は神様からのエール

　米国で中華料理店に行くと食後に、「おみくじ」の入ったクッキー（フォーチュン・クッキー）が出る。「占い」ごとが好きなのは洋の東西を問わない。日本では神社や寺院で「おみくじ」を売っている。おみくじにはいろんな種類があるが、一般的なのは「大吉」から「大凶」までを数段階に分けて表示し、それにしたがって健康や恋愛、金運、勝負運などの個別項目を占っているタイプだ。結果が良ければ喜ぶと同時に有頂天にならないようにと自戒し、悪ければ「次には好転する兆し」と肯定的に考えるべきだという。読み終わったおみくじは持ち帰らずに、境内に設けた専用の柵や樹木などに結びつける。神様との"縁"が結ばれたという意味である。ちなみにこのおみくじの70％は、山口県周南市にある女子道社という会社が作っている。

第4章
Chapter 4

つき合い
Social Events

お中元／お歳暮	❶	Mid-year and Year-end Gifts
上座／下座	❷	Seating Etiquette
宴　会	❸	*Enkai*: Parties
あいさつ	❹	*Aisatsu*: Greeting People
年賀状／暑中見舞い	❺	Greetings Cards at New Year and in Summer

① Mid-year and Year-end Gifts
お中元/お歳暮

Expressing your thanks with practical gifts

Many Japanese people are shy, and find it difficult to convey their feelings of **affection** and thanks through words. Maybe that's why we try to do so through giving gifts. The sale of *ochūgen* (mid-year) and *oseibo* (year-end) gifts derives from the custom of giving gifts to superiors and customers established in the Edo period, when businesses serving this custom thrived.

Ochūgen is the term used for gifts given between July 1 to 15, and those given in August around the beginning of autumn according to the old lunar calendar are called *shochū mimai*, or inquiries after one's health in midsummer. From then until the end of the month they are called *zansho mimai*, inquiries after one's health in the lingering summer heat.

Oseibo, on the other hand, refers to the etiquette for the year's end, when the offerings to the souls of ancestors were distributed as New Year gifts to family, neighbors, and people who helped you. The usual *oseibo* gift was salted salmon.

モノに託して感謝の気持ちを伝える

シャイ（恥ずかしがり）な人が多い日本人は、**愛情**や感謝の心を言葉で伝えるのが苦手である。そのためかモノを贈呈することでその気持ちを伝えようとする。江戸時代には上司や得意先に贈る風習が定着し、この贈呈文化に目をつけた商売も盛んになり、それが今日の「お中元セール」「お歳暮セール」に繋がっている。

「お中元」は7月1日から15日までに贈る場合の呼び名で、それを過ぎて8月の立秋（7日前後）前までなら「暑中見舞い」、それ以降の月末までなら「残暑見舞い」となる。

一方、「お歳暮」は年末に交わす儀礼のことで、先祖の霊に捧げたものを新年の供え物にと、近所や実家、お世話になった人などに配るものだった。お歳暮の定番は塩鮭だった。

Chapter 4 Social Events

② Seating Etiquette
上座／下座

Seating arrangements for the host and guests decided by social hierarchy

When being shown into a drawing room, getting into a car, or sitting down for a meal at a traditional restaurant for business negotiations, Japanese people pay close attention to their social status in comparison with the other parties in order to decide where they should sit. Abroad you have at most the "ladies first" rule, but in Japan there is the custom for host and guest to consider their relative status in terms of relationship, position and age to decide whether to take one's place in a position of greater or lesser honor, and to offer even just a slightly better seat to each other.

In a Japanese style room, the place of highest honor is that closest to the *tokonoma* alcove. The place of least honor was by the door. In an elevator, the place of honor is furthest inside, while the spot by the button panel is the spot of least honor; in taxis the seat behind the driver is the place of honor, and least honor beside the driver; and in trains the window seat facing the direction of travel is the place of honor, with your back to the direction of travel is least honor. Even within these general outlines, the positions are ranked. It seems terribly complicated, but generally the seats of honor are in the most comfortable and safest seats in an emergency, while the least comfortable and most convenient seats to come and go in the service of your superiors are the positions of least honor.

主客・上下の人間関係で決まる座席

　商談で応接間に通される、車に乗る、料亭の座敷に座るといった際に、互いの人間関係を見て、誰がどこに座り、自分がどこに座るべきかをひどく気にするのが日本人である。海外ならせいぜいレディファーストのマナーがあるくらいだが、日本では主客の関係、役職・年齢の上下関係などを見て「上座/下座」を決めたり少しでも上位の席を譲り合ったりする習慣がある。

　日本風の座敷なら上座は「床の間」の近くになる。そして入口に近い場所ほど下座になる。これがエレベーターの中だと操作ボタンのある奥側が上座で、操作ボタンの前が下座になり、タクシーでは後部座席で運転席の後ろが上座、運転席の隣が下座になる。電車などでは進行方向に向かって窓側が上座、後ろ向きの通路側が下座になる。その中間の場所にもそれなりのランクがある。ややこしいようだが、快適で万一の際の安全度が高いほど上座になり、快適でなくても何かの用事ですぐ出入りしてゲストや上司に貢献できそうな場所が下座という点では一貫性はある。

エレベーターの中
Inside an Elevator

操作ボタン

電車の中
On a Train

窓

進行方向

タクシーの中
Inside a Taxi

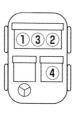

日本料亭で
At a Japanese Restaurant

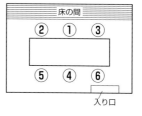

床の間

入り口

3 *Enkai*: Parties
宴会

The important role of *kanji* (organizer)

The parties held on celebratory occasions, such as a wedding reception, or to entertain a business client are called *enkai*. In a traditional Japanese *enkai*, the *kanji* plays an important role, dealing with everything on behalf of the host, from arranging the **venue** and the catering, contacting the **participants**, and seeing to the welcome and send-off, to directing the proceedings and settling the bill.

The *kanji* must have a firm **grasp** of the order of proceedings and the rank of the guests. He must also consider who to ask to propose the **toast**, and what kind of entertainment to offer. In the case of a **felicitous occasion** such as a wedding reception, he should also consider what words to use, such as using *ohiraki ni suru* instead of the word *owaru* (finish) to signal the end of the party.

進行役である「幹事」の大切な役目

結婚式の披露宴に代表される祝い事や大事な商談相手の接待などのために催されるパーティが「宴会」である。日本の伝統的な宴会で重要な役目を果たすのが「幹事」である。幹事は、**会場**や料理の手配、**参加者**への連絡、送迎の手配、宴の演出さらには会計までのすべてを、ホストに代わって取り仕切る。

幹事は、宴の進行順序や賓客たちの序列を**把握**していなくてはならない。**乾杯**をするにしても、誰にその「音頭」をお願いすべきか、どういった「余興」が用意されているかも考えておかねばならない。ことに披露宴のような**めでたい席**では、言葉の使い方にも気をつかい「終わる」を「お開きにする」などと言い換えられなくてはならない。

Chapter 4 Social Events

Aisatsu: Greeting People
あいさつ

Deciding the angle of a bow

Greeting a person of high rank with lowered head and back bent in a bow is not limited to the Japanese, but *ojigi* (bowing) seems to foreigners to be a very Japanese custom. It's true that Japanese people bow a lot, and few people shake hands. Japanese books on etiquette even include a guide to the angle of the bow for different occasions.

The angle of the most formal bow is 45°. For a first meeting, it is 30°, while a general greeting to acquaintances and colleagues is 15°. There is still a culture of precisely formulating your bow according to your status in relation to the other person.

If you want to experience the most formal bow **at close quarters**, the staff at the entrance to a hotel or department store will oblige.

「おじぎ」の使い分けに出る秩序意識

　貴人に挨拶するのに、頭を下げ腰を曲げておじぎする（bow）のは日本人だけの風習ではないのだが、外国人の目にはとても「日本人的」に映るようだ。たしかに日本人は誰に対してもよくおじぎをする。握手するひとは少数だ。それに、マナー本に、「おじぎの角度を使いわけるように」と書かれているのも日本ならではだ。

　つまり相手に対する最上級のおじぎは上体を45度の角度にする。初対面の挨拶程度なら30度。知人や同僚との軽い挨拶なら15度などと書かれている。相手と自分との関係を秩序意識で考え、細かく形式化する礼儀作法の文化がまだ残っている。

　身近なところで最上級のおじぎを受けたければデパートやホテルの入り口などで従業員がしてくれる。

Chapter 4 Social Events

⑤ Greetings Cards at New Year and in Summer
年賀状 / 暑中見舞い

4 billion cards are sent at New Year

The custom of sending written greetings at New Year is not a new one. In the Edo Period they used to be delivered by messengers, but these were replaced by the post office system introduced during the Meiji Period. From 1935 special stamps were printed at New Year, and 1949 saw the introduction of New Year postcards featuring a lottery number (with various prizes being awarded in a draw), a practice still followed today. In 1996 over 4 billion of these cards, called *nengajō*, were printed. The number being sent has decreased with the increasing popularity of email and cell phones, but even so, in January 2013 the number of *nengajō* sent reached 3.6 billion. That's about thirty cards for every person in the country.

Following on from the success of New Year cards, summer greetings postcards known as *shochū mimai* went on sale, but they didn't really catch on, and only about 240 million are sent each year (about two for every person).

40億枚のはがきが行き交う新年

新年の挨拶に書状を交わす習慣は新しいものではない。江戸時代には飛脚がそれを運んだという。明治以降、飛脚は郵便制度に変わり、昭和10 (1935) 年から年賀切手が発行されるようになった。昭和24 (1949) 年には現在に続く「お年玉付き年賀はがき」(抽選で景品がつく) が発行されるようになり、平成8 (1996) 年には発行枚数は40億枚を超えた。電子メールや携帯電話の普及などでその数は減ってきているものの、それでも2013年1月に行き交った年賀状の数は約36億枚にのぼる。国民1人あたり約30枚だ。

年賀状の成功に後押しされて、夏の「暑中見舞い」はがきも売り出されたが、こちらは利用者がそれほど伸びず、発行枚数2億4000万枚 (国民1人あたり約2枚)。

Chapter 4 Social Events

第 5 章
Chapter 5

衣・食・住
Clothes, Food, and Homes

着物・小物 ❶ Kimonos and Accessories
和　食 ❷ Japanese Food
家 ❸ Homes
暮らし方 ❹ Lifestyle

Kimonos and Accessories
着物・小物

The *furisode* worn by unmarried women

The word "kimono" ordinarily means clothing, but it is sometimes used to mean traditional Japanese wear, that is, the word kimono as used in English, especially to refer to women's wear. This includes the eye-catchingly glamorous *furisode*. There are certain conventions in kimonos and *furisode*. First of all, for both men and women, the left flap of the kimono neckline (as seen by someone facing you) should never be on the outside. This is the opposite of Western-style women's wear. It is called *hidari-mae*, and it is the way used for dressing the dead, so is seen as bringing bad luck. The long-sleeved *furisode* is worn by unmarried women around the age of twenty, while married and older women wear the *tomesode*, which has shorter sleeves and a relatively **subdued** pattern.

「振袖」は未婚女性が着る

　衣類を意味する普通の言葉「着物」は、時として伝統的な日本の衣装つまり「和服」、とくに女性たちの「お召し物」だけを意味する。なかでもあでやかさで人目をひくのは「振袖」である。その「和服」や「振袖」にもちょっとしたしきたりがある。まず襟合わせだが、男女とも（相手から見て）左手側の襟を外側に出して着ることはない。女性の洋服の場合と逆である。これは「左前」といって死者の着付け方であり、運気が傾く不吉なものとされる。また、袖の長い「振袖」は20歳前後の未婚女性が着る。既婚者や年齢を重ねた人の場合は袖の短い、図柄も比較的**地味な**「留袖」を着る。

The family crest imprinted on formal wear

Formal wear for occasions such as weddings and funerals, usually a *haori* for men and a plain black *tomesode* for women, is imprinted with the **family crest**, called a *kamon*. This can be on the back, sleeves, or chest, and the greater the number (1, 3, or 5) imprinted indicates a higher social status.

Unfortunately, however, fewer people are wearing kimono these days, and they have the image of being something only worn on formal occasions, or something for high-class people to wear. A more casual, everyday version might be the light cotton *yukata*, which is an item of summer clothing, and is provided by Japanese inns for sleeping in. Originally it was worn when visiting a bathhouse.

礼服には「家紋」をつける

　結婚式や葬儀など改まった場所に着ていく礼装として、男性は羽織に女性は黒地の「留袖」などに、その家の「**家紋**」がついたものを着る。これを「紋付き」というが、背中、胸元、袖など紋をつける数（1・3・5）が増えるほど格式が高い。

　だが着物を着る日本人は残念ながら減っている。「あらたまった場で着るもの」とか「高級なものを身に付けるべき」といったイメージが定着したからだ。もっとカジュアルで、身近に接する機会としては、旅館で寝巻きとして出されたり、夏の衣料して用いられる「浴衣」だろう。もとは入浴時の着物だった。

Chapter 5 Clothes, Food, and Homes

Essential accessories for kimono

One essential accessory that women cannot do without when wearing a kimono is the *obi*, or sash. Since the mid-Edo period, the most popular has been a wide *obi* with a **sumptuous** design or unusual weave, with over ten ways to tie it. Before then, the *obi* had only been about 10cm wide and worn closer to the hips.

Long ago wearing a short sword stuck through the *obi* at the hip conferred an air of dignity on men, but after it was forbidden to do this they had to make do with a folding fan instead. Women also keep their fan in their *obi* near the breast. Incidentally, the small folding fan is apparently a Japanese invention.

Another small accessory that goes with a kimono is the *tenugui*, a multipurpose cotton towel. Others include the *kinchaku*, a small drawstring bag for keeping personal items in, the *noshibukuro* gift envelope, the *fukusa* silk cloth used for keeping things like tissue paper in, and the small scented sachet that women keep at their breast.

着物に欠かせぬ小物類

着物に欠かせぬものといえば、女性の場合には「帯」がある。**華麗な**図柄や変わった織り方をした幅の広い帯が普及し、10を超える結び方が生み出されるようになるのは江戸時代の半ばから。それまでは10センチ幅程度で、締める位置ももっと腰に近かった。

男性の場合、昔なら脇差（小刀）を腰にさすことで威厳をもてたが、帯刀禁止の現代では、手に持つ「扇子」程度しかない。女性はこれを帯の胸元にさしたりする。ちなみに小さく折りたためる「扇子」の仕組みは、日本人が発明したものだといわれている。

他にも着物に似合う小物としては、用途万能の木綿タオル「手ぬぐい」。身の回りの小物を入れる小さな袋で口元を紐で締める「巾着」、「のし袋」や懐紙などを入れるハンカチのような「袱紗」、女性が胸元に挟む小さな「匂い袋」などがある。

2 Japanese Food
和食

Special affection for rice

The usual word for a meal is *gohan*. This refers to a meal made from a grain such as rice that has been boiled or steamed. For Japanese people, a meal consists of boiled or steamed grain, and of all the grains rice has a special place in their affections. Until the Edo period rice was also used as a currency and to pay salaries.

In the old days, any children leaving grains of rice in their bowl uneaten would be scolded by their parents as a matter of course. The kanji for rice (米) is made up of the characters 8–10–8 (八十八), which is the number 88, and children were told that this meant the farmer took eighty-eight steps and efforts to make that rice, so it was wrong to waste even one grain. Those parents also had in mind that they themselves were unable to enjoy white rice for all three meals. This was partly due to **poverty** and **food shortages** after the war, but in any case people were not in the habit of eating white rice every day. Even in farming families, they often ate various other grains and **tubers**.

米に対する格別の想い

食事を意味する普通の言葉として「ご飯」という。これは米など**穀物**を炊くか蒸すかした食品のこと。日本人にとって食事とは穀物を蒸すか炊くかしたものであり、穀物の中でも米には特別な愛着を持つ。江戸期まで米は通貨であり、給与でもあった。

子供たちが茶碗に「ご飯」の粒を付けたまま食事を終えようとすると、昔の親たちは必ずこう注意した。「お米という字は、八十八と書く。これはお百姓さんが八十八もの手間をかけてお米を作るという意味だから、ひと粒でも無駄にしたらバチが当たる」と。その親たちには、「自分たちは三食とも白米は食べられなかった」との思いがあった。**貧困**や戦後の**食料不足**も影響しているが、そもそも庶民が白米を日常的に食べるという習慣がなかったのだ。農家でさえ雑穀や**イモ類**が多かった。

A step up from the sushi restaurant experience

These days, children going to a sushi restaurant where the chef is on standby for orders are surprised not to see ready-made dishes circulating on a conveyor belt as in a *kaitenzushi* bar. These have become the standard and what I am about to explain is unnecessary for them. However, for those who want to enjoy a "real" sushi restaurant, let me just give four examples of things to watch out for.

1) You should start with the **milder flavor** ingredients (such as white fish), and save the stronger flavors and pickled items for last.
2) Respect seasonal and local produce. The shop will want to show it off.
3) Eat it as soon as it's placed before you. Sushi quickly dries out and loses flavor. Oh, and don't drench it in soy sauce. Don't bite it in half, but eat it in one mouthful.
4) Don't use the restaurant's **jargon**. *Oaiso* for the bill, *agari* for more tea, *murasaki* for soy sauce, *gari* for ginger, *sabi* for wasabi, and so on were all originally jargon used by the staff, and sound **uncouth** and **vulgar** when used by a customer. I'll leave it at that.

「すし屋」体験のステップアップ

　最近の子供は、板前が待ち受けるすし屋に行っても「お皿が回ってないね」と不思議がる。回転寿司が普及し、「すし屋」の世界標準になってしまうと以下の話は無用になる。しかし、「ちゃんとした店」で楽しみたい人のために心得として4つほど書いておこう。
　①すしネタを食べる順序は「**うす味**」（白身など）から。味の濃いもの、酢締めの光りものは最後に。
　②旬のもの／地物を尊重して。店が自慢したいネタである。
　③出されたらすばやく。寿司はすぐに乾いて風味が落ちる。おっと、しょうゆの付けすぎも禁物。二つに食いちぎろうとせず一口で。
　④店の"**符丁**"は使わない。「お愛想」（会計を）、「あがり」（お茶を）、「むらさき」（しょうゆ）、「がり」（しょうが）、「さび」（わさび）などは、本来、店側の符丁だった。客が使うのは**野暮**かつ**下品**である。　以上。

Does eating *hatsumono* extend your life?

Japanese people have long enjoyed marine and land **produce** as it is harvested and are particularly sensitive to the idea of *shun* (season). *Shun* means literally "ten days," and food is said to be truly delicious and at its best for just ten days. In the Edo period, right at the beginning of the season the people would call the first time an item reached market *hatsumono* ("**first crop**"), and would buy it even for a high price on the **justification** that it would "extend your life by seventy-five days." Bonito, rice, tea, soba noodles, **bamboo shoots**, eggplants, sake and so forth were popular. In the Edo period, the first bonito of the season could fetch a ridiculously high price of at least 100,000 yen for a single fish. Even when the government banned the practice, it didn't stop.

But why seventy-five days? There doesn't seem to be any reason for this, although it is also said that, "Rumors persist for seventy-five days."

「初物」を食べると寿命が延びる？

　四季折々の山海の**産物**を楽しんできた日本人は、「旬」に敏感である。「旬」とは10日という意味なので、ものごとの盛り、食材の本当においしい期間はわずか10日ほどということになる。江戸時代の庶民は、その旬が始まってすぐ、初めて市場に出る食材を「初物」と呼び、これを食べると「寿命が75日延びる」と**言い訳**しながら、多少高い値段でも手に入れようとした。カツオ、米、茶、ソバ、**たけのこ**、ナス、酒などが人気だった。江戸時代には「初鰹」1尾に10万円以上の値がつく過熱ぶり。幕府が禁じてもとまらなかった。

　ところで、なぜ「75日」なのか？　根拠はない。「人の噂も75日」などともいう。

The Correct Way to Hold Chopsticks 箸の持ち方

Japanese food is eaten with chopsticks. In ancient times chopsticks resembled tweezers, being made from a folded-over strip of bamboo. Today's practice of using two separate sticks apparently dates from the Nara period, and the throw-away *waribashi* sticks came in during the Edo period. Traditionally eating was intimately linked with religious ritual, so there were various rules governing table manners. These included how to hold chopsticks, and even now there are many families who are strict about teaching this to children.

　和食は箸を使って食べますが、古代の箸はピンセットに似た竹製の折り箸でした。現在のように２本に分かれた箸を使うようになったのは、奈良時代頃からと言われ、江戸時代には使い捨ての割り箸が考案されました。古来、食事は神事と密接な関係があったため、食事作法についてさまざまな約束事がありました。中でも、箸の持ちかたや使いかたについては、今でも子供達に厳しいしつけをしている家庭が多いのです。

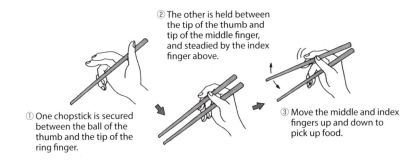

② The other is held between the tip of the thumb and tip of the middle finger, and steadied by the index finger above.

① One chopstick is secured between the ball of the thumb and the tip of the ring finger.

③ Move the middle and index fingers up and down to pick up food.

① 箸の一本を、親指の腹と薬指の先で固定させる。
② もう一本を、親指の先と中指の先で挟むようにして、上から人差し指を添える。
③ 食べ物をつまむ時は、人指し指と中指を上下させる。

How to hold bowls 器の持ち方

Japanese cuisine is said to be a feast for the eyes as well as the mouth. Thoughtful attention is given not just to the taste of the food, but to its presentation on the dish and the dish itself. Unseemly manners should therefore be avoided when eating. The basic rule is to lift a dish in order to eat the food it contains. You should place your fingers under the dish to lift it, and then place the dish on the palm of your hand. You should never grab hold of a dish by the rim. Also, it is good manners to replace the dish in its original position after eating.

日本料理は「目と口で味わう」と言われます。料理の味だけでなく盛り付けや器にも、細やかな気配りがされているのです。そのため、食べるときにも見苦しくない作法が求められます。器に入った料理は、器を手に持って食べるのが基本です。その場合は、器の底に指を差し入れて持ち上げ、手のひらに乗せるようにしましょう。器の口をつまんで持ち上げるのは禁じられています。なお、食べ終えた器は、元と同じ位置に戻すのが作法です。

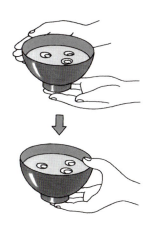

3 Homes
家

Tatami rooms partitioned by *shōji*

All around the world people have **distinctive** ways of building their homes, striving to make the most comfortable and strongest home they can with the materials available to them, which also determine their lifestyle. The oldest known houses in Japan were the **pit dwellings**, while in the fourteenth century the *shoin zukuri* style modeled on the study spaces of zen monks came in, and in the fifteenth century the *sukiya zukuri* followed the aesthetics of the tea-ceremony room. Residences that initially were only available to powerful samurai or high-ranking priests over time became popular with ordinary people.

There is no clear definition of a Japanese style home, but most people probably have an image of tatami floors, rooms partitioned by *shōji* and *fusuma* sliding doors, a *tokonoma* alcove set into the wall, and a veranda facing onto the garden. Without fixed furniture like a desk or bed, the room sizes are flexible.

畳に座り、障子で仕切る暮らし方

　世界中の民族がそれぞれに**個性的な**家を作ってきた。手近な材料で作れて、できるだけ頑丈で、できるだけ快適な家をめざして。それは暮らし方の反映でもあった。**竪穴式住居**から始まった日本人の家は、14世紀頃には禅僧の書斎に模したという「書院造り」が生まれ、続く15世紀には趣味的な茶室の雰囲気を取り入れた「数寄屋造り」も生まれた。当初は有力な武士や高僧の住まいだったものが時代とともに庶民の間にも普及した。

　「日本的な住宅」に明確な定義はないが、畳を敷き詰め、襖や障子で部屋を仕切り、壁の一部に「床の間」をしつらえ、庭に面して縁側を置くような空間をイメージする人が多いだろう。机やベッドを置かず、部屋の広さは変えられるようになっている。

Don't step on the border of the tatami or the doorsill!

There are certain **conventions** in Japanese houses. Children have it drummed into them not to step on the border of the tatami or the **doorsill**. One theory for this is that they traditionally mark the boundary of a sacred space, although another more practical theory holds that it was to protect a part that was easily damaged. Incidentally, you shouldn't stand on floor cushions either. Guests sit on them so it's rude to do so.

踏んではいけない畳の縁や敷居

　住む上での**しきたり**もある。子供たちは、畳の縁や**敷居**を踏んではならないとしつけられる。理由は、それらが神聖な空間を守る境目「結界」と考えられたからという説がある。また傷みやすい部分だから大切にしたという説も合理的である。ついでにいえば座布団も踏んではならないものだった。お客が腰を据えるものだから失礼になる。

Genkan entrance 玄関

You enter through a sliding door that clatters as you open it. You take off your footwear and step up on to the raised wooden floor called the *agariguchi*. It is good manners to rearrange your shoes so the toes are pointing towards the door.

　ガラガラという音を立てる引き戸を開けて入る。履き物を脱いで、一段高い板張りの「あがり口」に上がる。脱いだ履き物は、つま先を入口の方に向けて揃え直すのが礼儀。

Washitsu Japanese-style rooms 和室

Rooms are laid with tatami mats, the number of which determine the room size of the room, as in 6-mat rooms, 8-mat rooms and so forth. Old Japanese houses were devised so that sliding doors could be removed to create larger rooms as necessary.

畳敷きの部屋で、その数によって６畳間、８畳間などと呼ばれる。古い日本家屋の場合は、必要に応じて各部屋を仕切る襖を取り外すと、広い部屋になるという工夫がこらされている。

Japanese-style toilets 和式トイレ

Unlike Western toilets, on which you sit over the bowl, in Japanese toilets you squat over the bowl with your back to the door. Men can stand over them to urinate. For people used to Western-style toilets, they can come as a bit of a shock.

便器に腰を掛ける欧米式と違い、和式は入口を背にして便器に**またが**り用を足す。男性の小用は立ったまま行う。欧米式に慣れた人には、ちょっとしたカルチャーショックだ。

Tokonoma alcove 床の間

The *tokonoma* is an alcove slightly raised from floor level in which an ornament or flower vase is placed, with a painting or piece of calligraphy hung on the wall. They can be seen in tearooms, and even a Japanese-style room in a new house will have a *tokonoma*.

床を一段高くして置物や花瓶を置き、壁に書画などを掛ける。茶室にもみられるもので、新しい日本家屋の和室の一室は必ず床の間つきになっている。

Furo bath 風呂

In old Japanese houses even the bath was made of wood, but nowadays these have all but disappeared. However, the way of bathing remains unchanged, and you should never wash yourself while in the tub.

古い日本家屋は風呂も木製だったが、現在はめっきり見かけなくなった。しかし、入浴法は昔のままで、身体を洗う時は浴槽から出て洗うのが日本流である。

Shōji paper screen 障子

These are screens made of a wooden frame onto which washi paper is pasted, and they are good for allowing in natural light and keeping the room warm. They are unique to Japanese houses.

木組みをほどこした戸に和紙を張ったもので、自然の採光や室内の保温に適している。日本家屋ならではの独特の工夫である。

Amado shutter 雨戸

These are shutters that are opened during the day and stored away in built-in compartments, and pulled closed to cover windows at night. They are called *amado*, or "rain doors," since they used to be kept closed on rainy days, but now their main function is to prevent burglaries and maintain privacy.

日中は収納しておいて、夜は「戸袋」から引き出して使う。雨の日に閉めたことから「雨戸」というが、現在は防犯やプライバシーを守ることが主な役目になっている。

Oshiire cupboard 押入れ

These are the large built-in cupboards in Japanese-style rooms where bedding and items not in daily use are stored. In the past children used to hide in them when scolded by their parents.

寝具や日常使わないものの保管場所として、和室に付設されている。昔の日本の子供は、親に叱られると、ここに逃げ込んだものだ。

Bedding 寝具

This is the bedding used in a Japanese-style room. All Japanese people used to sleep on a futon mattress laid out on the tatami. At night, the living room was thus quickly converted into a bedroom.

和室に布団を敷いて寝るのが、昔の日本人の一般的風習だった。夜になると、和室は寝室に早変わりする。

Butsudan Buddhist altar 仏壇

Even today, many people start the day by putting their hands together in prayer before the family's Buddhist altar containing the ancestral memorial tablet.

先祖の位牌を祀った仏壇に向かって手を合わせ、一日のスタートをする日本人が多い。

Kamidana Shintō altar 神棚

Most households involved in trades such as shopkeeping, farming, or fishing keep a shrine dedicated to their patron god.

商売をしている家、農家、漁師の家などは、たいがい神様を祀る神棚を設けている。

Kotatsu heated table こたつ

The whole family gathered around a warm *kotatsu*—a low table heated from below and covered by a quilt—used to be a typical winter scene in Japan. Family breakdown is perhaps not unrelated to the fact that the *kotatsu* has largely been replaced by central heating.

家族全員がこたつに入って暖をとるのが、日本の冬の当たり前の家庭風景だった。家庭崩壊は、暖房の発達でこたつが不要になったことと無縁ではないのかもしれない。

Lifestyle
暮らし方

Life is ordered around the head of the family

The house reflects the lifestyle: who lives there and how determines how the space and contents are used. In Japan, the whole way of life is ordered around the head of the family, who is either the father or the householder fulfilling that role. He sits in the seat of highest honor, is served more elaborate meals, and is the first to take a bath (everyone takes turn using the same bathwater). It was only in the twentieth century (in the Taisho period) that the scene of a happy family sitting around the dinner table began to be seen.

家長を中心に作られる秩序

　家は暮らし方の反映である。誰がどんな風に暮らすかで、空間や道具の生かされ方が決まる。日本では家長を中心に暮らし方の秩序が作られてきた。家長は父親あるいはその役を担う世帯主である。家長は上座に座り、食事も特別のお膳で一品多いし、風呂に入るのも一番先（湯を使い回すから）。一家が同じ食卓を囲んで団欒（だんらん）するような光景が生まれるのは20世紀（大正時代）になってからである。

Seiza and *agura*

Since there aren't any chairs, you have to sit on the tatami or wooden floor. *Seiza*, or kneeling with your bottom resting on your heels, is the way women and priests sit as well as the position used for formal situations. The informal sitting position is cross-legged—sitting with your bottom on the floor and your legs folded in front of you. This is called *agura* in Japanese, and is written 胡座, literally "barbarian sitting." The peoples of the countries to the west of China, such as Iran and Mongolia, were called "barbarians" and the term is thought to be derived from this. *Seiza* is part of the relatively new etiquette that developed after tatami became popular, whereas before that the norm was to sit cross-legged, *tatehiza* (sitting with one knee drawn up), or *yokozuwari* (sitting with your legs folded to one side).

正座とあぐら

　椅子がないのだから、畳か板の間に座るしかない。正座つまりあらたまった場合や僧侶や女性たちの座り方は、「屈膝座法」。脚を折り曲げ尻がかかとの上に来るように座る。一方、くつろいだ座り方は「あぐら」。尻をついて座るが脚を投げ出さず引き寄せる。「あぐら」は「胡座」と書く。イランやモンゴルなど中国西方の民族を「胡」と呼んだが、そこから伝わったとされる。正座は畳が普及するようになり、礼儀作法などが細かくなった後世のもので、むしろ「あぐら」や「立てひざ」「横座り」の方が普通だった。

Frugality and *mottainai*

If I were to sum up the traditional Japanese lifestyle in one word, it would probably be "**frugality**." Society made a virtue out of **simplicity and economy**. People never bought unnecessary items and took care of those they had, repairing them when they broke or using them for different purposes to get the utmost out of them. Everything was recycled, from old clothes to ashes from the stove and human waste, and there were even specialist traders dealing in these. Methods of cooking and preserving food were also developed, with pickles and fermented foods like miso and soy sauce forming the basis of Japanese cuisine.

Within this frugal way of living, the word *mottainai* (What a waste!) came to be a **stock phrase**. It is rooted in Buddhist terminology lamenting the **transience** of things, with *mottai* referring to items in their original form, and *nai* to their non-existence. The word *mottainai* has now come to symbolize the lifestyle of those who are against the mass-consumerism prevalent in our current society.

つましさと「もったいない」

　日本人の伝統的な暮らし方をひとことでいうなら「つましさ」だろう。質素倹約を心がけ、それを美徳とする社会だった。無駄なものは買わず、ものを大切にし、壊れても修理するか転用して使い切る。着古した衣類はもとより糞尿からかまどの灰まで役立つものであり、専門の買取り業者もいた。食べ物の調理法、保存方法も発達し、漬物や味噌・醤油などの発酵食品は日本食の基本でもある。

　こうしたつましい暮らしの中で人々の口癖になっていたのが「もったいない」だった。ルーツは仏教用語で、ものの本来のカタチ「物体」がなくなる無常さを嘆く言葉だったという。「MOTTAINAI」は、大量生産・大量廃棄の現代社会に反発する人たちの暮らし方を象徴する世界語でもある。

Chapter 5 Clothes, Food, and Homes

第 6 章
Chapter 6

日本人のこころ
Soul of Japan

和	❶	Harmony
型	❷	Form, Way of Doing Things
気	❸	Energy
情	❹	Feelings
忠	❺	Loyalty
神	❻	The Gods
仏	❼	Buddhism

1 Harmony
和

Harmony

While the Chinese character for *wa* means "harmony," it is also used to mean "Japan." For example, Japanese cuisine is known as *wa-shoku* and Japanese clothing is known as *wa-fuku*.

"Harmony" is a basic value defined as the ability of people to cooperate and work together well.

Japan is a country whose traditions developed out of an **agricultural society** where people were forced to work closely together on a limited amount of land. In order to maintain this type of society, the needs of the village were more important than the needs of the individual, as all labored together to plant the rice and harvest the crop.

Therefore, as opposed to hunter- or immigrant-based societies, where a high value is placed on the power or actions of the individual, a society developed in Japan where the value is placed on understanding those with whom one must interact and on **taking action in groups**. That is the definition of *wa*.

和

「和」とは、そのまま訳せばharmonyである。

「和」はまた日本を表す別の表現でもある。たとえば日本食のことを、日本人は和食ともいう。日本の伝統的な服は和服と呼ぶ。

「和」とは、人と人とがいかに心地よく、共に過ごし、働くかということを表す価値観である。

日本は伝統的に、限られた土地を皆で耕作して、生活をしてきた**農耕社会**によって成り立っていた。この社会を成り立たせるためには、村人が自らのニーズよりも、村全体のニーズを考え、他の人々と行動を共にして稲を植え、収穫をしなければならない。

したがって、日本には、個人の力量や行動を価値基準の中心におく狩猟社会や移民社会とは異なる、常に相手との絆を気遣い、**グループで行動する**ことをよしとする価値基準が育まれた。それが「和」という価値観なのである。

Chapter 6　Soul of Japan

Lobbying

In order to preserve harmony (*wa*) when going "**on the record**" with an opinion, the Japanese will cautiously **share** information with others after careful consideration of the place and the timing. A very typical Japanese form of communicating one's will in this situation would be *nemawashi* (literally "**loosening the roots**").

If one presents a proposal for the first time right at a meeting, there is a risk that one's superiors or others affected by the proposal will have a different opinion. Avoiding this risk by consulting prior to the meeting with key persons and adjusting one's proposal as necessary is called *nemawashi* ("**lobbying**").

It is common for *nemawashi* to take place **outside the office**, perhaps over dinner or while playing golf or at some other private setting (*ba*).

Through the repetition of *nemawashi*, there will naturally be fewer conflicts, with better sharing of plans and ideas.

根回し

人との「和」を保ち、賢く自らの意見を**公で発表**するために、日本人は適切な「場」を選び、「間」も考慮して慎重に人とその情報を**共有して**ゆく。こうした日本人の行動様式の典型が「**根回し**」という意思伝達方法なのである。

会議の「場」でいきなりプレゼンテーションを行うと、場合によっては上司や関係者と意見の対立を生むリスクがある。それを避けるために、関係する人に事前にその情報を伝えたり、必要に応じて提案内容を調整することを「根回し」という。

「根回し」は**非公式**であるのみならず、時には夕食やゴルフなどの会合といった職場から離れたプライベートな「場」で行われることもある。

そして、「根回し」をしっかりと**繰り返すことで**、人と公然と対立せずに、情報が共有され、企画やアイディアに関する情報が共有されるのである。

2 Form, Way of Doing Things
型

Etiquette

Sahō means doing what fits into the right *kata* ("form"). Just as Westerners greet each other with a handshake, so do the Japanese have their accepted forms of behavior when they meet each other. The etiquette of the Japanese today reflects practices that have been in place since feudal times.

For example, in the case of the tea ceremony, every act is carefully **choreographed**, from where people sit, to how the water is boiled, to how the tea is prepared, and so on.

Again, in the business world, one can observe *sahō* in action as the seller employs polite language and bows often as he shows various forms of respect to the buyer. Another case would be the social setting of a company, where a subordinate will use particular *sahō* with his boss.

For most Japanese, *sahō* is an **ingrained** pattern of behavior that affects their day-to-day actions without them even being aware of it. However, for people who come from overseas, some of these practices may appear puzzling. Why is someone bowing so many times in a particular setting? Or at another time, why is someone sitting **ramrod straight**? But for the Japanese, they are simply following the *sahō* that is appropriate for that place and circumstance.

作法

「作法」は、まさに「型」にのっとっている。

ちょうど、欧米の人が握手をする習慣があるように、日本では人と対面し、交流するときに日本ならではの習慣に従って行動する。そして、日本には封建時代以来受け継いできた様々な習慣が、現代社会の人間関係にも投影されているのである。

たとえば、茶道において、どこに客人を案内し、どのようにしてお湯を沸かし、お茶を点て振る舞うか、全て**定められた方式がある**。

また、ビジネスの世界では、ものを売る側が買う側に対して、敬語を使い、より深くお辞

儀をするなど、様々な敬意を表すための作法がある。また、会社では上司と部下との間で、部下が上司に対してどのように行動するかという作法がある。

　多くの日本人は、自分が目に見えない作法に従って、行動様式を変化させていることすら、それがあまりにも**当たり前すぎて**、気づかないかもしれない。しかし、海外から来た人が日本人をよく観察すると、不思議に思える行動を発見する。なぜ、ここで何度もお辞儀をしているのか。どうしてこの人は**背筋を伸ばして**固まったようにして座っているのかなど。場所や状況に応じて、日本人はそうした作法に従っているのである。

Discipline

In certain cases, it may be necessary to spend many years **in training** to master *kata*. Only then, after the *kata* has been mastered, does the student really first understand the true logic of his movements, and then from there he may further develop his skill.

This demanding process of learning a *kata* is called *shūren*. *Shūren* may be seen in the business world in the relationship between subordinate and boss, although in recent years the example of the boss who manages his subordinates harshly without any feedback has become rarer. That said, Westerners who have Japanese bosses are still often **puzzled by** the lack of feedback.

It is true that this lack of feedback is different from the communication and management style in the West.

修練

「型」の習得には時には何年もの**修業**期間が必要となる。そしてしっかりと「型」を学んだ後に、はじめて学習者はその合理性に気付き、そこからさらに技量を発展させてゆく。

この「型」を学ぶ厳しい過程を「修練」という。そして、「修練」というものの考え方は、ビジネスのノウハウを習得してゆく上での、上司と部下の関係にもみてとることができるのだ。フィードバックがなく、ただ厳しく指導する上司は、最近でこそ少なくなった。とはいえ、今なお、欧米人が日本人を上司にもったとき、フィードバックの少なさに**戸惑う**ことがよくある。

確かに、このフィードバックの少ない日本流の指導方法は、欧米のマネージメントとは根本的に異なっているようだ。

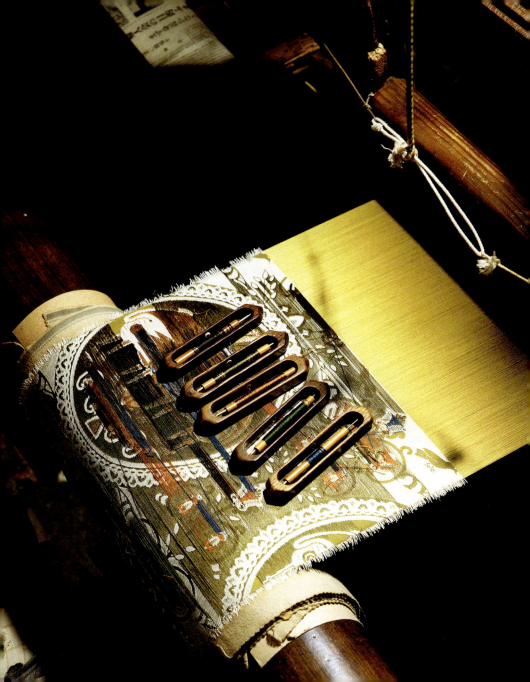

3 Energy
気

Air, Atmosphere

Kūki ("air") is not simply a physical phenomenon. In English as well, "air" is also used to describe the atmosphere of a situation.

As in the Japanese phrase *kūki wo yomu* ("reading the air"), the conditions that have brought about a particular atmosphere or situation are said to be the *kūki*.

The Chinese character of *kū* in *kūki* is the character for "sky" and also means "**empty**." The character for *ki* is combined with the character for "sky" or "empty," to form *kūki*, or "air." **Putting it another way**, *kūki* is not merely a physical phenomenon; it also includes all of the various energies that **inundate** a particular situation.

As part of **getting along in life**, the Japanese will always try to determine what particular energies (*ki*) are coming to play in a situation and do their best to take appropriate action based on that.

Ki is the energy that is created by the **interchange** between people. Therefore, most Japanese feel that it is important to do their best in understanding the circumstances of the people around them in order to create good *ki*.

空気

「空気」は単に気体のことだけを意味しない。英語でも、「空気」は雰囲気などを示すときに使われる言葉である。

そして、日本語の場合も「空気を読む」という言葉があるように、人がコミュニケーションをするにあたって、そこでの雰囲気や様子が醸し出す状況を「空気」という言葉で表現する。

「空気」の「空」は、何もない**からっぽな状態**を示す漢字である。そのからっぽな状態に「気」

が混ざり、「空気」となるのである。**言葉を換えれば**、「空気」は単なる気体ではなく、そこに**充満する**様々なエネルギーをすべて包括したものということになる。

　そこに充満しているのが、どのような「気」なのかを察知し、それをもとに適切に物事に対処することは、日本人が常に心掛けている**処世術**ともいえよう。

　「気」は人と人とが**交流**する中で生み出されるエネルギーである。したがって、「場」や人の立場などを理解し、よりよい「気」をつくろうと多くの日本人は考えているのである。

④ Feelings
情

Personal Feelings

It is the willingness to embrace the love of all people **without question as to their nationality**. It also means that there is a sympathy for those whom one comes into contact with who have not been so fortunate in their lives. These emotions that one has for others are called *ninjō*.

For example, if a court is trying a criminal, the judge may **give a lighter sentence** if the person in question committed the crime **due to the unfortunate circumstances of his environment**. In that case, it would be said that the judge had been moved by *ninjō* and people would applaud his decision.

It is true that it is difficult for most Japanese to accept the idea that "business is business" and separate their personal feelings from business. Although business should be conducted in a manner in which ideas are objectively exchanged and judgments made on that basis, in Japan it is instead common to conduct business on a "heart-to-heart basis," and this can often lead to broken relationships and bad business deals.

Of course in Japan, the **principle** of not mixing business with one's personal feelings also exists. When one is faced with someone taking an opposing position, however, one takes *ninjō* into account and is careful to do what one can to **accommodate** that person.

人情

　洋の東西を問わず、人は誰でも親しい人に対して愛情を抱いている。また、めぐまれない人に接すれば、たいていの人には同情心がうまれる。この、他の人に対する個人的な感情を「人情」という。

　たとえば、刑事裁判で、被告人が**不幸な境遇にあったが**ために罪を犯したであろうと思われる場合、判事が**軽い判決を下す**ことがある。この場合、判事は「人情」によって心を動

かされたとされ、人々はその判決に拍手するというわけである。

　実は、日本人は、「ビジネスはビジネス」として、個人の「情」とビジネスを切り離すべきものだという考えになかなか馴染めない。本来は客観的に意見を交換し、判断を行うべきビジネスでのやりとりが、日本では「ハートとハート」のやりとりとして受け取られ、それがもとで人間関係が上手くいかなくなったり、取引が不調におわることもある。

　もちろん、日本でもビジネスと個人の情とを混同してはいけないという**道徳律**は存在する。それだけに、人は反対意見を述べたりするときは、「人情」を意識し、気を使い、相手の**立場をたて**ながら表明するのである。

Obligation, Duty

Giri means the responsibility and effort that go into **maintaining** a relationship between one person and another.

For example, if one is **indebted** to another for a favor done, then it is said that one has *giri* to the other person. In that case, Japanese ethics require that one be well aware of the *giri* incurred and **repay the favor**.

In Japan this type of connection from person to person has traditionally been strong. Especially during the feudal Edo Era, one's position was strictly fixed according to one's rank, sex, age, and so on. It was not possible to **deviate from** one's rank or make an attempt to better oneself within society.

Because of this, conflicts between one's obligations (*giri*) and one's feelings (*ninjō*) were a common theme in the **traditional performing arts** such as the *kabuki* or *bunraku* ("puppet theatre"). An example of such a conflict would be a daughter who became engaged to one man to fulfill her *giri* to her father, while her true affections (*ninjō*) were for another young man. This would be a classic *giri-ninjō* theme.

義理

「義理」とは、人と人とが人間関係を**維持して**ゆくための義務や務めを意味する言葉である。

たとえば、ある人に大変**お世話**になった場合、その人に対して「義理」があると人はいう。そこで生まれる義理を意識して、受けた**恩恵に報いる**ことが道徳的に求められているわけである。

日本の場合、この人と人との縛りが伝統的に強かったといえよう。特に、江戸時代に代表される封建時代には、身分や性別、そして年齢など、様々な立場での役割が厳しく設定されていた。そして、役割**を逸脱する**ことや、自らの立場を超えて行動することは禁じられていたのである。

したがって、「義理」に縛られながら、その縛りを超えた人と人の「情」との間に挟まれて葛藤するテーマが、歌舞伎や文楽などの**伝統芸能**でよく取り上げられた。たとえば、親の「義

理」に縛られて婚約させられた娘と、その娘が本当に恋する若者との物語などが、それにあたる。「義理」と「人情」というテーマである。

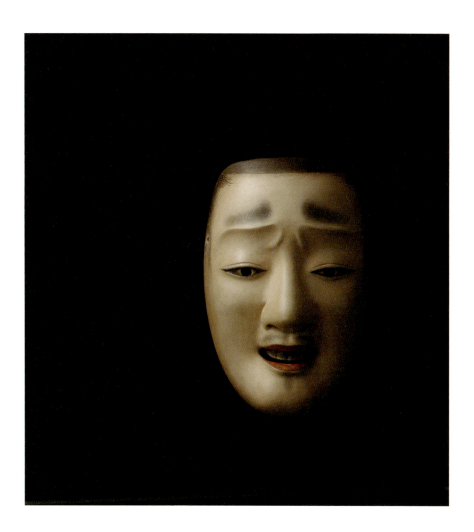

Social Debt

The social value known as *on* has heavily influenced the concept of *giri* ("obligation").

In the feudal period, a lord would pay his samurai a **stipend** and guarantee their position in society. It was the usual practice to guarantee that rank not just to that particular samurai, but to his descendants as well.

Having received a position and the guarantee of a living, the samurai would have incurred *on*, and in order to repay that social debt, the samurai would loyally serve his lord, at times having to **put his life on the line**. In other words, this was the samurai's *giri* ("obligation").

Even today, people often speak of "**having *on***" to a particular person. Common examples would be the *on* that is incurred by a child to his parent, or a student to his teacher, or an employee to his boss.

It is expected that those who incur *on* will make efforts to repay it. In most cases, *on* and *giri* are lifelong obligations, not something which affects one only for the short-term. In the old days, forgetting to repay one's *on* was considered a very **unethical** act and would be heavily criticized.

恩

　「義理」という考え方に最も影響を与えるのが「恩」という価値観である。

　封建時代には、君主は自らの部下である侍に**俸禄**を与え、その侍の身分を保障する。その地位は、その侍一代ではなく、代々受け継がれることが普通であった。

　この身分と生活の保障を君主から受けることが、侍にとっての「恩」である。侍はその受けている「恩」に報いるために、時には**命をかけて**君主に仕えなければならない。すなわちそれが侍の「義理」というわけである。

　現在でも、「**あの人には恩がある**」と人はよく言う。自分を育ててくれた親への「恩」、知識を与えてくれた教師への「恩」、そしてスキルを教えてくれた上司への「恩」などがそれにあたる。

人は「恩」に対して、それに報いるように努力することが求められる。

「恩」と「義理」との関係は、一時的なものではなく、多くの場合一生その人の人間関係に影響を与える。昔は「恩」を忘れることは、最も**非道徳的な**こととして、非難されていたのである。

Inside and Outside, Social Circle

When one is able to navigate the *shigarami* ("barriers") of a relationship and understand the particulars of *jō* ("feelings") versus *giri* ("obligations") to the point that one can let one's guard down and truly trust that person, then it is said that that person is *uchi* ("inside").

For example, a person who is not within one's family or close associates at one's company would be considered to be *soto* ("outside"), and one would **have some reserve** in dealing with that person until one got to know the person better.

How to distinguish between *uchi* and *soto* depends on the situation in question. For example, people in the same village who are not in the same family would be considered *soto* in terms of family, but those same people would be considered *uchi* in terms of the village versus people from outside the village. In Japanese, a foreigner is literally called *soto no hito* or *gaijin* ("outside person"). In this case, if we take Japan to be *uchi* ("inside"), then foreign countries must be seen as *soto* ("outside").

To reduce the risk of dealing with the **complications** of relationships, the Japanese have traditionally tended to only really open up to share information and personal feelings with people whom they felt were *uchi* ("inside") their social circle.

In order to be welcomed "inside" (*uchi*), it is necessary that two persons know each other well both **publicly and privately**. Then they will be in a position where they can open up to their feelings (*jō*) as persons "inside" the same social circle and freely share information.

内と外

人と人との複雑なしがらみの中で、その人の「情」と「義理」との関係がわかり、心を許して話ができる信頼関係が構築されたとき、その人は自分の人間関係の「内」にいると考える。

たとえば、家族や会社の親しい同僚は「内」の関係で、そこに入らない人は「外」の人と捉えられる。「外」の人とは、ある程度お互いがよく知り合うまで、率直な付き合いを**控える**のである。

この「内」と「外」との境界線は、その人のおかれている立ち位置の違いによって変化する。

たとえば、同じ村の人でも、家族からみると「外」の人ですが、違う村の人と比較すれば、「内」の人となる。外国の人を「外人」と呼ぶが、この場合は日本を「内」と捉えているので、外国は「外」に他ならない。すなわち、「外人」とは「外の人」という意味なのである。

複雑な人間関係から発生する**齟齬や軋轢**といったリスクを軽減するために、日本人は伝統的に「内」と考える相手に対してのみ、本当の思いや情報を共有する傾向にある。

「内」に迎えられるためには、何よりも、お互いを**公私ともに**よく知り合う必要がある。そして、「情」をもって話し合える関係になれば、「内」に入った仲間として情報が共有されるのである。

True Feelings and Facade

Two words that most closely represent the relationship of *uchi* ("inside") and *soto* ("outside") are *honne* and *tatemae*. *Honne* refers to the true feelings that are spoken by those who are "inside" (*uchi*) the same group, while *tatemae* is what is spoken **for show** or to be diplomatic.

For those who understand the Japanese communication style, it is relatively easy to see the difference between what is *honne* and what is *tatemae*. However, it is quite common for non-Japanese people to hear what is *tatemae* and misunderstand it as *honne*, later being surprised when things don't progress as they had thought they would. Unfortunately for those who cannot tell the difference between *honne* and *tatemae*, misunderstandings may sometimes arise where it is felt that the Japanese are not telling the truth.

In order to get the true intent (*honne*) of a Japanese person, one will be expected to become a member of his "inside" (*uchi*) group or go through someone who is inside the group.

本音と建前

「内」と「外」との関係を最も象徴的に表した言葉が、「本音」と「建前」である。「本音」とは、「内」の同じグループのメンバー同士で語られる本当に思っている内容のことで、「建前」は、**表向きの**、あるいは外交的なメッセージや言葉を指す表現となる。

日本人ならではのコミュニケーションスタイルを理解している人同士であれば、「本音」と「建前」とを見分けることは比較的簡単かもしれない。しかし、外国から来た人は、「建前」を聞いて、それを「本音」と勘違いし、あとになって思うように事が進まずにびっくりすることもしょっちゅうある。残念なことに、この「本音」と「建前」を理解していない人から見れば、あたかも日本人が嘘をついているように誤解することもあるかもしれない。

日本人から「本音」のメッセージを受け取るには、「内」に入ること、あるいは相手の属する「内」に加わる人を通して間接的に情報をとることが求められる。

Chapter 6 Soul of Japan

5 Loyalty
忠

Barriers

Japan's **vertical society**, with its highly varied types of relationships such as *me-ue, me-shita, senpai, kōhai, dōki,* and so on is quite complicated, and requires one to constantly make choices as to communication style. The Japanese call these types of **complicated relationships** *shigarami*.

The word *shigarami* originally refers to a device used to stop the flow of water. The word took on its broader meaning in the sense that a person's freedom to act was restricted by the *giri* ("obligations") that he would incur.

The use of the word *shigarami* to **refer to** the difficulty of relationships reflects the common practices of this **inflexible** society, which have developed over a long period of time.

However, at the same time it must be said that *shigarami* is a positive social value since it prevents people from acting **for selfish reasons** and instead encourages them to carefully consider the position of others.

しがらみ

「目上」、「目下」、「先輩」、「後輩」、「同期」、そして親子など、日本社会を彩る様々な**縦の構造**は、ある意味とても複雑で、それに対応するコミュニケーションスタイルも多岐にわたる。そんな**複雑な人間関係**を日本人は「しがらみ」と呼ぶのである。

「しがらみ」とは、元々水の流れを止める設備のことを意味する。これが、複雑な人間関係を表現する言葉となったのは、人間関係が生んだ様々な「義理」に縛られて人間の自由な行動が束縛されるからに他ならない。

日本人が、自らの人間関係のことを「しがらみ」と**表現する**背景には、長い歴史の中で培われた様々な常識や**硬直した**社会制度に、日本人そのものがとらわれていることを示していることになる。

しかし、同時に、「しがらみ」は、人が**自らの勝手で**行動するのではなく、相手の立場や気持ちを考えてどのように動くかを判断させる、大切な価値観でもあるのだ。

6 The Gods
神

The Gods

When Japanese refer to *kami*, they usually mean the gods of the **Shintō religion**, which has been in Japan since ancient times.

From the north to the south throughout Asia, it is possible to find religions that **worship** rocks and other objects in nature and that perform **purifying** rites with water. For the Japanese, who worshipped the mystery symbolized by nature, purifying one's body and soul before these objects was an important **religious rite**. With this objective in mind, various types of ascetic training in the mountains developed.

Unlike Christianity or Buddhism, there is no worship of **idols** in Shintō, where the worshipper is always at one with nature; the only exception to this would be mirrors used to reflect the symbols of nature.

Unlike Christianity, where people are expected to **atone** to a god for their sins, the appeal of Shintō for the Japanese is to be found in the respect paid to nature and, through being unified with the purity of nature, to in turn become pure oneself.

神

日本人にとっての「神」とは、多くの場合、日本古来の宗教である**神道**での様々な「神」を意味する。

実際、石や自然物を**崇め**たり、水で**清め**たりする宗教行為は、北から南までアジア全般でみることができる。日本人にとって、そうした自然を象徴する事物の神秘を崇め、その前で身や心を清めることが、大切な**宗教上の行為**だったのである。神道は、こうした目的のために山にこもって修行し、鍛錬する山岳信仰などをも育む。

キリスト教や仏教などと違い、**偶像**を信仰の対象とせず、常に自然と向かい合うことが神道の特徴で、唯一例外として「神」の象徴として自然を映し出す「鏡」などが崇拝されることがある。

　キリスト教とは違い、日本人にとっての「神」とは、人が自らの罪や**贖罪**を意識して対峙する「神」ではなく、自らを取り巻く自然への敬意と、清らかな自然に向かい、自らをも清めてゆく考えの中で創造されたパワーなのだ。

Purification

The act of **purifying oneself** before rocks, trees, and other objects of nature where spirits and gods reside is considered to be very important.

Such an act of purification is called *misogi*. For those in particular who participate in the rites of Shintō, it is expected that they will purify themselves with water, always keeping themselves clean.

The act of *misogi* can be found in many different forms in the traditions of Japan. For example, throughout the country one can see people pouring water over themselves at various festivals; or one might see people jumping into cold ocean water on New Year's Day as they **pray for good health in the coming year**; or one might find people standing under a waterfall as part of spiritual training in the mountains. There are countless examples.

For the Japanese of old, it was important to **mark the distinction** between everyday life and the time one would spend before the gods by first properly purifying the body and soul. Even now, before entering a shrine to pray, one will wash one's hand and rinse out one's mouth. It is only after purifying himself that a Japanese will then pray to the gods for the welfare of his family or business.

禊(みそぎ)

岩や大木など自然の造物に魂や神が宿るとする神道において、最も大切とされる行為がそうした精霊に向かうにあたって、**身を清める**行為だ。

この身を清める行為のことを「禊」という。特に、神道などで、神のそばに仕える者は、水などで身を清め、常に清潔にしておくことが求められた。

この「禊」の行為が、その後様々な形で日本の伝統の中に残るようになった。たとえば、お祭りで体に水をかけたり、元旦に冷たい海に入って**一年の無病息災を祈ったり**といった行為が日本各地にみられる。さらに、今でも山岳信仰で、滝にあたって身を清める風習があることなど、例をあげればきりがない。

昔の日本人にとって、日々の生活の中に**区切りをつけて**、心と体を清め、改めて神に向かう行為は、生きてゆく上での大切な「けじめ」でもあった。今も、神社にお参りをする前は、神社の入り口や前にある水場で手を洗い、口をゆすぐ。その後で、日本人は神に向かって商売や家庭の平安を祈願するのだ。

Chapter 6　Soul of Japan

Defilement

A concept that is closely related to *misogi* ("purification") is *kegare* ("defilement").

Kegare refers to both the defilement of the body and the soul. One must be purified before standing in front of the gods in order to not present a defiled self.

Many countries have the traditional value of "**purity**" in their cultures. In Shintō, this concept of being pure in the way that a virgin girl or child is pure also exists.

In Shintō, it is believed that children have spiritual powers that adults do not, and traditionally, it was considered ethically important that a woman remain pure until her marriage.

For adults, who were no longer pure like children or virgins, they would try to **rid** themselves **of** their *kegare* at shrines or other places of worship.

Kegare was not simply a matter of being physically unclean; in looks; it also referred to the **wickedness** in a person's soul.

穢れ

「禊」と深く関わる概念が「穢れ」である。

「穢れ」とは、心身ともに穢れた状態を示す。神の前に立つとき、人は穢れのない状態でなければならず、そのために「禊」を行うのである。

純潔という言葉がある。これは世界の多くの国にある古典的な価値観であり、文化現象だが、処女であること、また子供のように純粋であることへの美学が神道における「穢れ」という発想の対極にもある。

実際、神道では子供には大人にない神的なパワーがあると信じられており、婚姻するまでの女性が純潔であることは、封建時代の道徳律などとあいまって、昔は大切なことであった。

子供のように純真ではなく、処女のように純潔ではない状態が穢れた状態とされ、人々は大人になってからも、神社などでそうした「穢れ」を**払おう**としたのである。
　「穢れ」とは、単に見た目が汚いということを超えて、**邪悪**な心を持つことそのものを指す言葉として捉えられていたのである。

7 Buddhism
仏

Pathos

In facing death and dealing with the **fleetingness of life**, an element of sentimentalism has developed in Japanese Buddhism.

In its origins, Buddhism was a religion and philosophy that dealt with the changing circumstances of humans and the universe, as people sought to return to their natural selves through **self-reflection** and the control of desires.

However, when Buddhism came to Japan and was faced with the conflicting realities of the middle ages, it evolved to meet the needs of those looking for salvation in the next world, and became more sentimental as it did so.

Cherry blossoms are one example. They bloom for only a few days in early spring before **being blown off** the trees. The sad beauty seen in this **transition** is what is meant by *mono no aware*.

No one knows when he will die. Particularly in the olden days, it was common to die suddenly at any age. As with the sad beauty of the brief life of the cherry blossoms, so it is with the *mono no aware* of the brief life of humans.

ものの哀れ

仏教は、人の死を見つめる宗教でもある。したがって、そこには**儚い人生**へのセンチメンタリズムが含まれている。

元来、仏教は、人や宇宙の移り行く姿を捉え、自らの欲望を抑えて自然な姿に心を戻してゆく**自省的な**宗教であり、哲学であった。

それが日本に伝来し、中世の矛盾の多い現世にあって、人々が来世に救いを求めるセンチメンタリズムへと変化していった。

たとえば、桜は春ほんの数日間花を咲かせ、あっという間に**散ってしまう**。この**移ろい**

の中に美学を見いだしたのが、「ものの哀れ」という美意識だ。

　人も、いつ死を迎えるか予想できない。特に昔は、子供でも大人でも、あっけなく「あの世」に旅立つ。それは桜と同じように哀れなもので、人の儚い人生に「ものの哀れ」という美学を見出したのである。

第 7 章
Chapter 7

その他
Miscellaneous

縁起かつぎ	❶	Attracting Luck
図　像	❷	Iconography
レジャー	❸	Leisure
趣　味	❹	Hobbies

1 Attracting Luck
縁起かつぎ

The miraculous power of salt to cleanse impurities

One important concept evident in all Japanese customs is that of *kegare* (**impurity**) and *kiyome* (**purification**). *Kegare* is when bad energy takes hold, and *kiyome* describes the processes and rituals to get rid of it. One thing that is often used in *kiyome* rituals is salt. After attending a funeral, purifying salt is brought out and scattered on people's clothes, and on the ground for them to walk on it with their shoes. Sumo wrestlers sprinkle salt in the ring to purify it, and forming piles of salt in the ceremony to purify a new building site also serves the same function.

It is easy to confuse this with the little conical heaps of salt in the entrances to traditional restaurants and other businesses, which have a very different meaning. This practice is said to be based on the story of the Chinese Qin emperor Shi Huang-ti, who would do the rounds of his 3,000 **concubines** in an ox cart, and one of his lovers had the foresight to place some salt beside her door for the oxen to lick so that they would come to her more often. It's a **talisman** to attract customers.

穢れをはらう「塩」の霊力

日本人のしきたりに共通している重要な概念の一つは「穢れと清め」である。不吉な気が取りつくのが「穢れ」であり、それを振り払う所作や儀式が「清め」になる。清めの儀式によく使われるのが「塩」である。葬儀に参列した後には「清めの塩」が配られ、服に振ったり靴で踏むなどする。相撲で力士が土俵に撒くのも、地鎮祭で塩を盛るのもこの「清め」である。

混同されがちなのは、料亭など商売の家が玄関口に三角錐に盛る「盛り塩」だ。これは意味がまったく違う。由来は中国の故事で、秦の始皇帝が3000人もの愛妾宅を牛車で廻っ

ていたのだが、ある愛人が、「牛は塩をなめたがる」と思いついて自宅の玄関先に盛り塩したら、始皇帝の牛車がしばしば立ち寄るようになったという。客を引き寄せる**おまじない**なのだ。

The "beckoning cat" and "bear's paw" to attract money and people

The *maneki-neko* (beckoning cat) and *kumade* (bear's paw, or lucky rake) are considered lucky for outlets in the service industry. The cat with its right front paw raised is inviting money, and with its left paw raised is inviting people. If it has both paws raised in a "banzai" salute, though, it will end in bankruptcy for the business. The *maneki-neko* has become popular around the world since about 1990. However, unlike in Japan, it shows its "welcome" invitation with the palm of the hand facing towards itself.

金と人を呼ぶ「招き猫」と「熊手」

　客商売で縁起が良いとされるものに「招き猫」と「熊手」もある。猫が右手（右前脚）をあげているのは金運を招き、左手は人を招くという。欲張って両手をあげて「バンザイ」すると倒産だというオチがつく。1990年頃から招き猫は世界中に広がった。ただし「ウェルカム」と招く際の手の動きが日本と逆で手の平が自分に向いている。

　「熊手」はまだ国際的とはいえないが、めでたい飾り物をたくさんつけた「熊手」を求めて、毎年「酉の市」に出かける人が多い。人も金もこれでかき集めたいからだ。

Chapter 7 Miscellaneous

Lucky animals and plants

There are also many auspicious animals. According to one saying, "Cranes live a thousand years, turtles for ten thousand years," while the word for sea bream in Japanese is *tai*, which matches the latter part of the word *medetai*, meaning "lucky." The owl is connected with the saying "He without hardship is untroubled" since the word for owl (*fukurō*) is homophonous with the word for "untroubled," while frogs (*kaeru*) are homophonous with the word "return" in the phrase "Lost objects and money will return." Lucky plants include the trio of pine, bamboo, and plum. The usual theory is that this is from the Chinese tale "Three Friends of Winter" (from *The Analects* of Confucious), but this is on the subject of people thriving in the harsh environment of winter, and doesn't especially mean they are lucky, which is a Japanese-style transformation. For celebratory occasions, there is a brand of sake named after them too.

Speaking of Japanese-style transformations, there is the *daruma*. This originates in the monk Bodhidharma who attained **enlightenment** in China after meditating before a wall for nine years. Now, however, it is a doll used as a piggy bank or to pray for victory in an election. Many are squat and round, weighted at the base so they always return to the upright position, and since they always rise after a fall are considered lucky. On the other hand, since they lack arms and legs, those who are powerless with zero assets are also described as a *daruma*. It's complicated.

おめでたい動物と植物

吉祥をもたらす動物もたくさんいる。「鶴は千年、亀は万年」もの長寿とされるし、「めでタイ」の鯛、「苦労がないから不苦労」のフクロウもいれば、「なくした金やモノが帰る」というカエルもいる。植物なら「松、竹、梅」だろう。これは中国の「歳寒三友」(論語)の話からだという説が一般的だが、厳しい環境(冬)でも凛として生きる人の生き方がテーマな

のであって、別にめでたい意味はない。日本的に変形された。祝い事にと、この名で売る酒もある。

　日本的変形というなら「ダルマ」がある。元は壁に向かって9年も座禅して**悟り**を開いた中国の達磨大師である。貯金箱や選挙の勝利祈願に使われる人形になった。ずんぐり丸くて底部を重くした「起き上がり」人形タイプが多いので、転んでも何度でも立ち上がる「七転び八置き」がめでたいのだという。だが「手も足も出ない」姿から、無力な資産ゼロ状態になることも「ダルマになる」という。ややこしい。

2 Iconography
図像

The *kamon* representing the clan

In films about Japan's Warring States period, you can see warriors going into battle brandishing a **banner** featuring the clan's *kamon*, or crest. This crest is also emblazoned on kimono, food products and lanterns, gravestones, *noren* curtains, and so on. It is the mark that shows the correct **lineage** and social standing of the family. A *kamon* that has one or more rings around it shows the different branches that were established separately from the main family. The imperial family's crest features the "sixteen-petalled chrysanthemum," while that of the Japanese government is the "five-seven paulownia" crest with seven blossoms on the center leaf and five on each side leaf (as on the 500 yen coin). On the front of the Japanese passport is the chrysanthemum, and on the photograph page is a five-three paulownia as used by the Ministry of Justice.

「家紋」は一族を表すマーク

　日本の戦国時代を描いた映画などでは、将兵たちが家紋をつけた**旗**を振りかざして合戦する。家紋は着物についていたり、食器や提灯、墓石、のれんなどにもついている。それぞれに由緒正しい**家柄**であることを示す一族（ファミリー）のマークである。同じような紋でも丸く囲んであるとか、その丸も２重であるとかで本家と分家など支族の違いを示している。天皇家にも「十六花弁の菊」があり、日本政府も中央に７つ、左右に５つの花房についた「五七の桐」を用いている（500円硬貨）。日本のパスポートには表面に菊、写真のページには「五三の桐」がついている。法務省所管だからだ。

Chapter 7 Miscellaneous

191

Why are Chinese lions paired with peonies?

There are many **iconographic images** with a particular meaning that have traditionally been used on painted *fusuma* doors, kimono, tattoos, and Japanese *hanafuda* playing cards, among other things. The pairing of a Chinese lion with **peonies** is one of these. The lion is the king of beasts, and the peony is the king of flowers. According to legend, even the strong lion was robbed of its strength by a worm it gave shelter to in its body, and the saying, "The worm in the lion's body" refers to a person in power embracing a **traitor** amongst his friends. It is said that the best means to kill the worm is with drops of the night dew from a peony blossom. The design shows the bravery and **invincibility** of a ruler.

A similar pairing is that of a tiger in a **bamboo thicket**. Even a beast so strong as a tiger is afraid of elephants, and so it hides in a bamboo thicket. If it manages to conceal itself, it will be saved from the elephant.

なぜ「唐獅子に牡丹」なのか？

　襖絵、着物、刺青、花札などには昔から意味のある図像が使われることが多い。「唐獅子に牡丹」の組み合わせもその一つ。獅子（ライオン）は百獣の王であり、牡丹は百花の王である。伝説では強い獅子でも体内に巣食う虫に体力を奪われることがある。「獅子身中の虫」は権力者が味方の中に反逆者を抱え込むことだ。その虫を殺すのに最適なのが、夜、牡丹から滴る花の露だという。王者としての勇壮さや意気軒昂ぶりを示す図柄である。

　似たような組み合わせに「竹林の虎」がある。強い獣である虎も象は苦手。竹林に身を潜めば象から身を守ることができる。

Chapter 7 Miscellaneous

3 Leisure
レジャー

Japan's national sport, Sumo, is a kind of Shinto ritual

Sumo is a combat sport that has been practiced since ancient times, and it is said that some of the *haniwa* figures excavated from **burial mounds** are modeled after sumo wrestlers. It was also one of the rituals held at the Imperial Court in Heian times. Much later, in the Edo period, it flourished as popular entertainment as daimyo became patrons of popular wrestlers. At that time sumo tournaments were held twice a year **in the open air** for ten days during fine weather.

Sumo customs are based on ritual. Wrestlers scatter purifying salt in the ring, stamp the ground in the ring to summon the gods, and at the beginning of the bout squat with their chests thrust out and their arms open wide to show that they are unarmed. The ring itself is a sacred space, and under the covered rings the pillars to the east, west, south and north are adorned with green, white, red, and black cloths. This based on the philosophy of the Chinese Taoist ideal topography of green=green dragon=spring=east, white=white tiger=autumn=west, red=red bird=summer=south, and black=black tortoise=winter=north.

In the Kokugikan stadium the **pillars** are omitted for the sake of the audience, but four tassels, one of each color, hang from the roof in their place.

日本の国技「相撲」は神事の一種

相撲は古くから行われた格闘技で、**古墳**から出土する埴輪にも「力士」(相撲取り)をかたどったものがあるという。平安時代には宮中で行われる神事の一つでもあった。また江戸時代には大名が人気力士の後援者になり、興行としても盛んになる。当時の相撲場所は年に2回、**野外**で晴天の日に10日間開催された。

相撲の所作は神事にもとづいている。土俵に清めの塩を撒いたり、「四股」を踏んで神霊を呼び出し、しゃがんで胸を張る「蹲踞」の姿勢から両手を左右に開いて武器を隠し持たな

いことを見せる……など。土俵自体が神聖な場所であるし、屋根を持つ土俵では東西南北の柱に青・白・朱・黒の布が巻かれる。これは中国伝来の「四神相応」の思想にもとづくもので、「青＝青龍＝春＝東」「白＝白虎＝秋＝西」「朱＝朱雀＝夏＝南」「黒＝玄武（亀）＝冬＝北」をそれぞれ意味している。国技館は観客のために柱がなく、屋根の下につけた房の色で「四神」を表現している。

Lively seasonal outings

As I already mentioned under *ohanami* blossom viewing, Japanese people have always enjoyed particular seasonal entertainments throughout the year. In spring there was cherry blossom viewing, in early summer people gathered **shellfish** on the beach at low tide, a practice called *shiohigari*, and at the height of summer, there were the magnificent fireworks display and the *kawabiraki*, or "river opening" held in Ryōgoku in Edo. This was a festival to mark the beginning of the boating season, during which people could enjoy wining and dining on pleasure trips up and down the river. Summer was also the season for the *tanabata* star festival, the *bon-odori* dance for the Obon festival, and **catching fireflies**. In autumn people enjoyed displays of dolls made out chrysanthemums and going to famous spots to enjoy the **autumn colors**. Even in winter, **people with refined tastes** would enjoy drinking sake while gazing out at a snowy landscape.

季節ごとの賑わいを見せる行楽

　日本人は、先に書いた「お花見」のように、四季折々の変化を娯楽として楽しんできた。春には桜の「花見」があり、初夏には遠浅の海岸で**貝**を拾う「潮干狩り」、夏には江戸・両国の「川開き」と盛大な花火見物。「川開き」には、船に乗って川を上り下りし、飲食も楽しむ川遊びが解禁される。夏には「七夕」「盆踊り」「**蛍狩り**」などもある。秋には菊で作った人形などを楽しむ催しに出かけたり、**紅葉**の名所に出かける「紅葉狩り」をした。冬でさえ、**粋人**たちは「雪見」の酒を楽しんだ。

4 Hobbies
趣味

Getting into useless pastimes

The Japanese word *dōraku*, which means pastime, has a nuance of denial, or of **self-deprecation**. Getting into womanizing is called *onna-dōraku*, fishing is *tsuri-dōraku*, being obsessed with the theater is *shibai-dōraku,* and being into clothes and style is *ki-dōraku*, while an heir to the family business who plays around and **fritters away his inheritance** without studying or doing anything useful is called a *dōraku-musuko*.

The phrase *Dōraku mo hodohodo ni* ("Pastimes in moderation too") serves as a warning against getting too swept away in such futile pursuits. It was originally a Buddhist word indicating the enjoyment of **attaining enlightenment** following ascetic training. *Zanmai* is another Buddhist word referring to a state of perfect spiritual concentration. These days, adding *zanmai* to a word enhances the meaning, so that *dōraku-zanmai* means "a life of pleasure and gaiety," while *zeitaku-zanmai* means "luxury and extravagance."

役に立たないことに夢中になる「道楽」

日本語の「道楽」という言葉には少し否定的あるいは自嘲的なニュアンスがある。女性との浮気に夢中になれば「女道楽」、釣りならば「釣り道楽」、芝居に夢中になれば「芝居道楽」、衣装や着こなしに凝れば「着道楽」、そして継承すべき家業にも勉学にも役立たないことに夢中になって**遺産を食い潰す**子供を「道楽息子」などといった具合。

こういう無益なことへののめりこみを戒める言葉として「道楽もほどほどに」という。本来、この言葉は、修行の末に**悟りを開く**ことの楽しみをさす仏教用語だった。同じような言葉に「〜三昧」というのがあり、この言葉ももとは仏教用語で、精神がもっとも集中している状態のことを意味した。最近では、道楽生活にふけることを「道楽三昧」、贅沢のし放題なら「贅沢三昧」というように言葉の元の意味を強調するために使われている。

Japanese people make everything into a "way"

Many Japanese people throw themselves into pursuits with extreme earnestness, and such people seek a high level of spirituality even in their hobbies. In *kadō*, the way of flower arranging, *chadō*, the way of tea, *kōdō*, the way of incense, and others, the skills were polished and made into a profoundly spiritual practice, and in no time these pastimes ended up being representative of Japanese culture.

This attitude of pursuing a "way" (*michi*, or *dō*) can also be seen in the martial arts, with jūdō, kendo, karate-dō and so forth, and led to the way of thinking called *bushidō*, or the way of the warrior. These have become more than hobbies, and are in fact a way of life and daily training, with their own philosophy and **aesthetic**. They have also probably been influenced by the teachings of **Lao-zi**, who held that the "way" approached the ultimate truth of the universe.

The trend to follow the spiritual way to this profound and eternal truth is not something of the past. People today, too, follow the *kaizen* philosophy of continual improvement in service and quality in business, and even in popular culture there are people who **advocate** the "way of ramen," and the "way of manga." Maybe these will lead to some future Japanese culture that will impress the world.

何事も「道」にしたがる日本人

　日本人は一面では、生真面目にものごとに取り組むところがある。こういう人は趣味の世界でも高い精神性を求めようとする。「華道」「茶道」「香道」などのように、所作を洗練させ、奥深い精神性を伴う体系にし、いつのまにか日本文化を代表するものに仕立てた。

　「柔道」「剣道」「空手道」など武術の世界でも「道」を追求する姿勢が見られ、「武士道」という考え方も生まれた。これらは趣味というよりも、日々の鍛錬であり、生き方であり、哲学や**美学**に通じているといえる。古代中国の思想家である**老子**が説いた「道」の教えは、宇宙の真理・真相に迫る道だったが、そうした影響があるのかもしれない。

永遠に続く奥深い真理への道を歩もうとする精神的な傾向は、過去の話ではない。現代人も職場においては品質とサービス向上のための「カイゼン」を続けているし、大衆文化の世界でも「ラーメン道」とか「マンガ道」を**提唱している**人たちもいる。こうした分野からも将来の、世界が感心するような日本文化が生まれるのかもしれない。

INDEX 索引

A

agricultural society 152
agura 146
all-white kimono 74
altar to the gods 12
Amado shutter 141
Attracting Luck 184
autumn colors 196
autumn Equinox 34
avarice 50
average life expectancy 60
awakening of insects 18

B

bamboo shoots 130
banner 190
barbarian sitting 146
barriers 172
bear's paw 186
beautiful chestnut moon 44
beckoning cat 186
betrothal money 68
black beans 14
blossom viewing 20, 196
bodhissatva 86
bon-odori dance 42, 196
boundary of a sacred space 136
bountiful harvests 90
bowing 114
bow twice, clap your hands twice, then bow once more 88
buckwheat 48
Buddha 84
Buddhism 180
Buddhist altar 142
Buddhist home altar 84
Buddhist services for mourning 82
Buddhist weddings 72
Buddhist word 198
burial mounds 194
Butsumetsu 78

C

calamity 64
carp streamers 28
catching fireflies 196
chant sutras 40
Children are in the hands of the gods until the age of seven 58
Chinese lion with peonies 192
chopsticks 132
Christian weddings 72
Chrysanthemum Festival 32
climbing to a height 32
coexistence of *Shinto* and Buddhism 86
Coming of Age 60
coming-of-age ceremony 60
commuter marriages 70
confucius 62
conventions 136
cowherd 30
Cranes live a thousand years, turtles for ten thousand years 188
crop yields 46
crowning ceremony, to fit boys with a traditional cap 60
cupboard 141

D

Day of Mankind 24
Day of the Dog 54
deep-fried tofu 90
defilement 178
deity 56
devil's tongue jelly 96
discipline 158
doctrine of yin yang 76
doctrine of yin yang and the five elements 36
Dolls Festival 26
doorsill 136
dōraku 198

dōraku-musuko 198
dowry 68
drawing room 108
dried bonito 68
dried squid 68
drinking sake while gazing out at a snowy landscape 196

earthly desires 34, 50
elaborate bridal robe 74
emperor's public renunciation of divinity 86
energy 160
engagement 68
enlightenment 188
epidemics 98
Equinoctial Weeks 34
etiquette 156
excellent 102

family altar 82
family crest 122
family registers 80
feeling 162
felicitous occasion 112
felicitous occasions 76
feng shui 62
festival floats 46
festivals 46
Fifteenth Night 44
fireworks 46

first bonito of the season 130
first crop 130
First Day of the Horse 28
First Day of the Snake 26
first shrine visit of the New Year 50
fish catches 46
five-seven paulownia 190
folding fan 124
Folk Beliefs 90
foreign import 86
Form, Way of Doing Things 156
fortune in and demons out 16
fortune telling 102
forty-ninth day 82
frugality 148
full-moon dumplings 44
funerals 76, 80, 88
furisode 120
futon mattress 142

gift envelope 124
god of fishermen 94
Gods 84
gongs 46
good business 90
grain 126
greed 50
Greetings Cards at New Year 116

Greetings Cards in Summer 116
guest of honor 74

haniwa figures 194
happy family sitting 144
harmony 152
harvest festival 44
herring roe 14
hinduism 94
hundredth day 82

iconography 190
impurity 184
inari fox deity 84
inquiries after one's health in midsummer 106
inquiries after one's health in the lingering summer heat 106
Inside and Outside 168
irises 28

Japanese cuisine 152
Japanese food 126
Japanese-style rooms 138
Japanese-style toilets 139
jargon 128
Jizō: god of children and local community 98
Jizō hall 98

jūdō 200

karate-dō 200
keeping things like tissue paper in 124
kelp 68
kendō 200
ki-dōraku 198
Kimonos 120
kneeling with your bottom resting on your heels 146
Kotatsu heated table 143

L

Lao-zi 200
Leisure 194
lineage 190
lobbying 154
longevity 32, 62
Long-life Celebrations 62
Lord Enma 96
loyalty 172
lust 50
luxury and extravagance 198

marine and land produce 130
maternity bands 54
Meiji Restoration 86
memento 74
memorial services 82
memorial tablet 82

Michizane's curse 90
mid-autumn moon 44
Mid-year Gifts 106
milder flavor 128
milky way 30
monk Bodhidharma 188
monotheistic religion 84
Moon Viewing 44
mottainai 148
mountain worship 100
Mount Fuji 100
movable national holidays 34
movement to destroy Buddhist temples and statues 86
mugwort 28
multipurpose cotton towel 124
mutual aid 80

national sport 194
natural heritage 100
Neither heat nor cold lasts beyond the equinox 34
New Year 12, 94
New Year postcards featuring a lottery number 116
New Year's Eve 48
nightlife business 90
non-religious ceremonies 72
numerous offspring 68

oath 70
obedient ears 62
obligation 166
obligation, duty 164
obon traditions 30
offerings 90
offertory box 88
old lunar calendar 44
1,000-year candy 58
one-year anniversary 82
onna-dōraku 198
order of proceedings 112
organizer 112
outings 196

P

pampas grass 44
paper lanterns 46
parties 112
pastime 198
Pathos 180
Peach Festival 26
Personal Feelings 162
pine decoration 12
pit dwellings 134
prayers 54
puppet theatre 164
pure land 82
purification 176, 184

R

reception 70
red padded vest 62
religious ritual 132
removing all the misfortunes of the year 50
rice brandy 32
rice dumplings wrapped in bamboo leaves 28
rice gruel with seven herbs 24
river opening 196
rumors persist for seventy-five days 130

S

sacred site 90
safe delivery 54
sake infused with herbs 14
salted salmon 106
sash 124
scaffold platform 42
season 130
seasonal festivals 22
second anniversary 82
seiza 146
Senbu (or *sakimake*) 78
Sengen Shrines 100
Senshō (or *sakigachi*) 78
Seven Lucky Gods 94
Shakkō (or *sekiguchi*) 78
Shakyamuni 90
shibai-dōraku 198
Shintō altar 143
Shintō belief 12
Shintō home shrine 84
Shintō ritual 194
Shintō weddings 72
shiohigari 196
shoin zukuri style 134
shōji and *fusuma* sliding doors, a *tokonoma* alcove 134
shōji paper screen 140
short sword 124
shrine 84
simplicity and economy 148
single moon viewing 44
sitting with one knee drawn up 146
sitting with your legs folded to one side 146
six lucky and unlucky days 76
sixteen-petalled chrysanthemum 190
sixth anniversary 82
small drawstring bag for keeping personal items in 124
small scented sache 124
social debt 166
soup containing mochi rice cakes and fish or chicken 14
soy sauce 128
special dishes prepared for New Year 14
spring and autumn equinoxes 18
spring equinox 34
squat 194
stacking boxes 14
stack of three sake cups of different sizes were filled three times 70
stalls 46
stamp the ground in the ring 194
star festival 30
starvation 98
stipend 166
strips of paper 30
sukiya zukuri 134
sumo 194
sushi restaurant 128

T

Taian (or *daian*) 78
talisman 56, 184
tanabata star festival 196
taoism 94
tatami floors 134
tea-ceremony room 134
temple 84
tenjinsama god 84
terrible 102
the bride's change of outfit 74
the cherry among flowers, the samurai among men 20
the first day of spring 16
the gifts given to guests to take home 74
the Gods 174
the hottest part of summer 36

the other world 34
the seventh day after death 82
the way of the warrior 200
the wedding ceremony 70
the worm in the lion's body 192
theocracy 86
thirteen celebration 60
thirty-second anniversary 82
this world 34
Three Friends of Winter 188
Three Sacred Treasures 12
tiger in a bamboo thicket 192
toast 112
tokonoma alcove 108, 139
tomesode 120, 122
Tomobiki 78
traditional performing arts 164
transience 148
treasure ship 94
true feelings and facade 170
tsuri-dōraku 198
twelfth anniversary 82
twenty-four divisions of the solar year 18

ukiyoe woodblock prints 100
uncouth 128
unfortunate occasions 76
unlucky years 64

venue 112
vestiges 32
viewing ratings 48
visit the grave 82
vulgar 128

wa-fuku 152
waka poems 100
ward off misfortune 22
ward off the misfortune 64
warrior dolls 28
water trough 88
way 200
way of flower arranging 200
way of incense 200
way of manga 200
way of ramen 200
way of tea 200
weaning ceremony 56
weaver maid 30
wedding reception 112
white dew 18
white fish 128
winding stream banquets 26
world heritage 100
worshipping Mt. Fuji 100

year-end gifts 106
yin-yang ideology 22
yukata 122

zen monks 134

あ

赤いちゃんちゃんこ 62
あぐら 146
暑さ寒さも彼岸まで 34
油揚げ 92
雨戸 141
天の河 30
泡盛 32
安産 54
家柄 190
一周忌（1年目）82
一神教 84
移動祝日 34
稲荷 84
戌の日 54
位牌 82
岩田帯 54
陰陽五行 36
陰陽思想 22
浮世絵 100
氏神様 56
うす味 128
宴の進行順序 112
打掛け 74
内と外 168
疫病 98
宴会 112
縁起かつぎ 184
えんま様 96
お色直し 74
応接間 110
大晦日 48
お食い初め 56
押入れ 141
おじぎ 114
お地蔵さん 98
お釈迦様 92
お正月 12
お歳暮 106
おせち料理 14
お中元 106
お月見 44
お年玉付き年賀はがき 116
お屠蘇 14
お花見 20，196
帯 124
帯料 68
お盆行事 30
おみくじ 102
恩 166
女道楽 198
陰陽道 76

か

会場 112
外来 86
加冠式 60
賀寿 62
数の子 14
型 156
片見月 44
鰹節 68
華道 200
門松 12
鉦 46
神 174
神棚 12，143
家紋 122
通い婚 70
唐獅子に牡丹 192
空手道 200
川開き 196
幹事 112
乾杯 112
気 160
飢餓 98
着道楽 198
記念品 74
旧暦 44
清め 184
義理 164，166
キリスト教式 72
金銭欲 51
巾着 124
熊手 186
栗名月 44
黒豆 14
慶事 76
啓蟄 18
穢れ 178，184
結界 137
結婚式の披露宴 112

下品 128
牽牛 30
剣道 200
元服式 60
鯉幟 28
孔子 62
香道 200
行楽 196
国技 194
曲水の宴 26
穀物 126
五七の桐 190
戸籍係 80
こたつ 143
古墳 194
混在 86
こんにゃく 96
昆布 68
婚約 68

さ

歳寒三友 188
賽銭箱 88
災厄 64
作物のでき具合 46
茶道 200
作法 156
三回忌 82
山海の産物 130
山岳信仰 100
三々九度 70

三十三回忌 82
三種の神器 12
残暑見舞い 106
寺院 84
塩鮭 106
潮干狩り 196
しがらみ 172
此岸 34
敷居 137
しきたり 137
色欲 51
「四股」を踏んで 194
持参金 68
獅子身中の虫 192
四十九日 82
耳順 62
自然遺産 100
地蔵堂 98
子孫繁栄 68
七福神 94
視聴率 48
質素倹約 148
芝居道楽 198
収穫祭 44
十五夜 44
十三祝い 60
十三回忌 82
柔道 200
重箱 14
秋分の日 34
修練 158

十六花弁の菊 190
旬 130
春分 18
春分の日 34
書院造り 134
情 162
正月 94
障子 134, 140
上巳の節句 26
浄土 82
商売繁盛 92
菖蒲 28
しょうゆ 128
食欲 51
暑中見舞い 106, 116
初七日 82
除夜 50
白身 128
白無垢 74
神事 133, 194
人日の節句 24
神社 84
神政一致 86
神前式 72
人前式 72
神道 12, 86, 174, 175, 176, 178
神道と仏教 86
すし屋 128
図像 190
ススキの穂 44

相撲 194
スルメ 68
政教分離 86
正座 146
成人 60
成人式 60
贅沢三昧 198
聖地 90
世界文化遺産 100
節句 22
浅間神社 100
扇子 124
禅僧 134
相互扶助 80
葬式 76
雑煮 14
葬礼 88
そば 50
蹲踞 194

た

大吉 102
大凶 102
宝船 94
たけのこ 130
山車 46
畳 134
竪穴式住居 134
立てひざ 146
七夕 196
七夕の節句 30

端午の節句 28
短冊 30
団欒 144
誓い 70
竹林の虎 192
千歳飴 58
ちまき 28
忠 172
中秋の月 44
弔事 76
長寿 32
長寿（賀寿）62
「手水」場 88
提灯 46
重陽の節句 32
月見団子 44
つましさ 148
釣り道楽 198
鶴は千年、亀は万年 188
手ぬぐい 124
天神様 84
伝統芸能 164
天皇の人間宣言 86
道 200
道教 94
登高 32
道楽 198
道楽息子 198
床の間 110, 134, 139
読経 40
留袖 120, 122

な

名残り 32
夏の土用 36
七回忌 82
七草がゆ 24
7つ前は神のうち 58
匂い袋 124
二十四節気 18
二礼二拍手一礼 88
人情 162
根回し 154
年賀状 116
農耕社会 152
のし袋 124

は

廃仏毀釈 86
羽織 122
白露 18
箸 132
旗 190
初鰹 130
初詣で 51
初物 130
花は桜木、人は武士 20
花火 46
埴輪 194
彼岸 34
引き出物 74
人の噂も75日 130

ひな祭り 26
百か日 82
賓客 74
ヒンドゥー教 94
風水 62
袱紗 124
福は内、鬼は外 16
富士山 100
富士山信仰 100
武士道 200
襖 134
符丁 128
仏教用語 198
仏事（法事） 82
仏前式 72
仏壇 82, 142
布団 142
振袖 120
文楽 164
平均寿命 60
豊穣 92
奉納 92
法要 82
豊漁の神 94
俸禄 166
菩薩 86
墓参 82
蛍狩り 196
仏 180
盆踊り 42, 196
本音と建前 170

煩悩 34, 51

まじない 56
招き猫 186
水商売 92
禊 176
道真のたたり 92
民間信仰 90
武者人形 28
無常さ 148
明治維新 86
めでたい席 112
もったいない 148
ものの哀れ 180
紅葉 196
桃の節句 26

厄年 64
厄除け 64
櫓 42
厄を払う 22
屋台店 46
野暮 128
浴衣 122
「雪見」の酒 196
横座り 146
よもぎ 28

立秋 106
漁の水揚げ高 46
老子 200
六曜 76

和 152
和歌 100
脇差 124
和式トイレ 139
和室 138
和食 152
和服 152

日本のしきたり
Customs of Japan

2016年 7月9日 第1刷発行

著 者　IBCパブリッシング編

発行者　浦　晋亮

発行所　IBCパブリッシング株式会社
　　　　〒162-0804 東京都新宿区中里町29番3号 菱秀神楽坂ビル9F
　　　　Tel. 03-3513-4511　Fax. 03-3513-4512
　　　　www.ibcpub.co.jp

印刷所　日新印刷株式会社

© IBC パブリッシング 2016
Printed in Japan

落丁本・乱丁本は、小社宛にお送りください。送料小社負担にてお取り替えいたします。
本書の無断複写（コピー）は著作権法上での例外を除き禁じられています。

ISBN978-4-7946-0418-7